I0585041

THE LUCIANIC MANUSCRIPTS
OF 1 REIGNS

HARVARD SEMITIC MUSEUM

HARVARD SEMITIC MONOGRAPHS

edited by
Frank Moore Cross

Number 51
THE LUCIANIC MANUSCRIPTS
OF 1 REIGNS
Volume 2
Analysis

by
Bernard A. Taylor

Bernard A. Taylor

THE LUCIANIC MANUSCRIPTS OF 1 REIGNS

Volume 2

Analysis

Scholars Press
Atlanta, Georgia

THE LUCIANIC MANUSCRIPTS OF 1 REIGNS
Volume 2
Analysis

by
Bernard A. Taylor

© 1993
Harvard University

Library of Congress Cataloging in Publication Data
Taylor, Bernard A. (Bernard Alwyn), 1944–
   The Lucianic manuscripts of 1 Reigns.

   (Harvard Semitic monographs; no. 50–   )
   Greek and English.
   Revision of pt. 2 of author's thesis (doctoral)—
Hebrew Union College-Jewish Institute of Religion, 1989.
   "The running text [of the Lucianic manuscripts of 1
Reigns] primarily consists of all the readings supported
by a majority of the family, and non-family"—V. 1, introduction.
   Includes bibliographical references.
   Contents: v. 1. Majority text — v. 2. Analysis.
   1. Bible. O.T. Samuel—1st.—Greek—Versions—
Septuagint—Criticism, Textual. I. Bible. O.T.
Samuel, 1st. Greek. Septuagint. 1992.
BS1324.G7S4 1992   222'.93048   92–36940
ISBN 1–55540–785–4 (cloth)

Printed in the United States of America
on acid-free paper

Contents

List of Tables

Glossary

Adaptation - The adjustment of the information in the Brooke-McLean second apparatus to conform to the **database** format. See pp. 17-22.

Addition - See **database categories**.

Antiochian Text - For 1 **Reigns** this term is synonymous with **Syrian Text** and **Lucianic Text**. However this is not necessarily true in other books. In the Pentateuch manuscripts boc_2e_2 are not Lucianic in the same sense as they are in 1 **Reigns**. See pp. 3-6, especially f.n. 12.

Archetype - The Greek text that lies behind related witnesses such as the Lucianic manuscripts, and to which they bear witness. See also **Vorlage**.

Base text - See **Database Categories**.

Characteristic - A distinctive feature (such as a form of a word, a word, or a phrase) that occurs in a manuscript or family of manuscripts. See also **trend**.

Collation manuscript - A selected manuscript to which other manuscripts are compared to ascertain their textual differences. In this study the term refers specifically to each of the two manuscripts to which other (selected) manuscripts are statistically compared to ascertain to what extent they share the collation manuscript's **characteristics**.

Common text - The body of **database** readings that are supported by a majority of all the manuscripts in the database. See also **variant**.

Critical apparatus - The second part of a **critical text** that lists alternative readings to those of the **running text** which are cited as the **lemma**.

Critical text - A reconstructed text intended to represent some aspect of the history or development of a manuscript, **family** or tradition. The text usually consists of a **running text** and a **critical apparatus**.

Database - A store of data accessible to a computer. For this study the term refers to the arrangement of the Greek material for 1 **Reigns** from the Brooke-McLean second apparatus in computer machine-readable form according to the standards established by CATSS. See pp. 15-27.

Database categories - The five divisions in the **database** into which the readings from the Brooke-McLean second apparatus are placed in order to represent the relationships between them and the Rahlfs text as **base text** (see pp. 22-27):

   a. **Base Text** - Readings shared in common with the Rahlfs text as the reconstructed exemplar of the **Old Greek**.

   b. **Omission** - A reading shorter than the base text. This category includes readings irrespective of whether or not the **base text** word ever actually formed a part of the "omitting" manuscript or its **archetype**.

   c. **Substitution** - A word or form of a word that differs from the **base text** reading. Because the point of reference is always the **base text**, **substitutions** to **additions** are consistently treated as **additions**.

   d. **Transposition** - Two or more words of the **base text** in a different order. See also **virtual transposition**.

   e. **Addition** - A reading longer than the **base text**.

Diplomatic Edition - An edition that prints a single manuscript as the **running text** and groups the **variants** of the other witnesses in the apparatus around the readings of the **running text**.

Doublet - One of two synonymous readings in the same context. The key to distinguishing doublets from dittography is that the former are synonymous while the latter are (essentially) identical. See p. 100.

Eclectic Text - A **running text** which consists of selected readings chosen according to predetermined criteria from among the readings of the witnesses, or where it is deemed necessary, from conjectural emendations.

Family of Manuscripts - A group of manuscripts that share distinctive readings in common over an extended passage or throughout a biblical book or beyond which set them apart from other manuscripts or groups of manuscripts. For a list of the families in 1 **Reigns** see p. 11.

Harmonization - The tendency for copyists to replace recensional readings with better known (non-recensional) **majority readings**. Because of the similarity to scribal emendation, harmonization is identified in this study on the basis of non-Lucianic manuscript support. See pp. 99-100.

Hexaplaric - There are two distinct uses of this term. The first use describes a manuscript as a descendant of the fifth column of Origen's Hexapla. The second use is as a term to describe a manuscript that has been contaminated, chiefly through marginal glosses, with readings either via the fifth column, or directly from one of the (from the perspective of the **Old Greek**) later translators: Aquila, Symmachus, or Theodotion.

Hexaplaric signs - The signs used by Origen to indicate passages that were in his Greek text but not his Hebrew text, or vice versa. Only two of the signs were utilized by Brooke-McLean in their text: the asterisk: ※; and the obelus: ÷.

Inner Greek variant - A **variant** that is deemed to have arisen within the transmission of the Greek text without influence from the Hebrew text. See also **letter variant**.

Integrated Text - A textual sequence in which the common elements from two or more extended **variant** contexts are combined to form one text with the remaining readings treated as **variants**. For the most part the Brooke-McLean apparatus is integrated, but at times they preferred to list several variant passages separately rather than integrate them, a format that was incompatible with the CATSS **database** format.

Καίγε text - The Greek recension identified (by Barthélemy) from its rendering of the Hebrew particle גם by the Greek καίγε. In extended passages in Samuel-Kings this later text has replaced the **Old Greek** text in most of the witnesses.

Kingdoms - See **Reigns**.

Lacuna - A portion of a manuscript missing due to physical damage. For a list of the passages missing from manuscripts in the **database** for this reason see p. 14.

Lemma - The word or words from the **running text** which serve(s) as a reference point in the apparatus around which to organize the **variants** in a **diplomatic** or **critical edition**.

Letter variant - A variation in spelling. This may have been intentional, or have arisen from confusion over such as vowels or diphthongs pronounced alike (itacisms), similar sounding consonants (such as δ/θ), or similar looking letters (such as Γ/T). See also **inner Greek variant**.

Lucian - The name 'Lucian' has been associated with manuscripts boc_2e_2 since the time of Ceriani (1861) due to the agreement between the text of these manuscripts and extant quotes in the writings of Syrian Church Fathers, especially Theodoret and Chrysostom. The use of the name is continued in this study for convenience in accord with accepted practice. See pp. 8-9.

Lucianic manuscripts [for Reigns] - As designated in the Cambridge Edition, with their equivalent in the Holmes-Parsons/Göttingen edition in brackets: b' (19), b (108), $b=b' + b$, o (82), c_2 (127), e_2 (93). For further details, see pp. 9-11.

Lucianic text - In **1 Reigns** the text of MSS boc_2e_2. Until this study the text has not been available outside of the Holmes-Parsons citations, the Brooke-McLean apparatus and Lagarde's attempted reconstruction.

Majority reading - A reading shared by at least a majority of the manuscripts under study, whether of the **database** manuscripts, or of the members of a **family** such as the **Lucianic manuscripts**.

Majority Text - A **critical text** for the study of a **family of manuscripts** within the larger context of the extant witnesses. The **running text** primarily consists of readings shared by at least a majority of the members of the family under study. Where there is no clear **majority reading**, that **minority reading** that best represents or accounts for the readings of the others is accepted, and placed in the running text within square brackets. The apparatus contains the variants of the family along with the list of the non-family members that support the reading.

Minority Reading - a reading supported by less than half the manuscripts under consideration, whether within the **database** as a whole, or within a **family of manuscripts**.

Octateuch - Genesis to Ruth (in English and Greek order, but not Hebrew order).

Old Greek - The original translations of the Hebrew Bible into Greek. For 1 **Reigns** Codex Vaticanus is accepted as the best witness to this text.

Omission - See **database categories**.

Proto-Lucianic Recension - The Greek text that underlay the fourth century work of the traditional **Lucian**. This term was coined to distinguish from the **Old Greek** because it was believed that Lucian's underlying text was itself a **recension** of the **Old Greek**. See p. 2, f.n. 4.

Recension - A text in which the differences are due to systematic intentional editorial revision.

Reigns - A translation of the Greek title Βασιλειων which designates the four books of Samuel and Kings in the Hebrew Bible. 1-2 Reigns correspond to 1-2 Samuel, and 3-4 Reigns correspond to 1-2 Kings.

"Rell" reading - Latin *reliqui:* "the rest"] An abbreviated listing used by Brooke-McLean to indicate that all the collated minuscule manuscripts not already listed for some other **variant** share the reading marked as "rell". See pp. 21-22.

Running Text - A text whose words follow continuously in their normal order in sentences, paragraphs and chapters. The alternative form is for the text only to be available as a list of **variants** in a **critical apparatus** or a **database**, as is the case with the **Lucianic manuscripts** in the Brooke-McLean apparatus.

Usually in a **diplomatic** or a **critical edition** a running text is printed at the top of the page and the **variants** are grouped in the apparatus(es) below. In the case of the **diplomatic edition** the running text is that of the selected manuscript, while in the case of the **critical edition** it is the **eclectic text** reconstructed to represent the selected form, or stage of the development of, the text that forms the running text.

Span - A series of three or more words cited in an apparatus by using only the first and last words separated by a dash as the **lemma** for the variants to that passage. See pp. 17-20.

Split reading - A reading that is shared by (only) half the manuscripts in a family. In this case there is no **majority reading**.

Standardization - The practice of conforming **variant** readings to one standard form. In this study the practice is limited to conforming the variant spelling of proper nouns in -ει- and -ι- solely to the latter in accord with the policy of both the Rahlfs text and the Göttingen editions. See p. 22.

Substitution - See **database categories**.

Syrian Text - See **Antiochian Text**.

Textual Stratum/Strata - Evidence in a text of recensional activity at a particular time, or at different periods of time.

Thackeray's Divisions of 1-4 Reigns - See pp. 31-32.

Transposition - See **database categories**.

Trend - A distinctive reading that sometimes occurs in a text or family of manuscripts, but not frequently enough to be a **characteristic**.

Variant - A difference in reading between two (or more) manuscripts. In the case of the **database** for this study it would be possible to regard the words that differ from the **base text** as the **variants**, but the **base text** does not merit such primacy, so the term is used to refer to any word in the **database** that is supported by less than a majority of the manuscripts under study, whether of the total **database** manuscripts, or of a **family of manuscripts**. See also **common text**.

Virtual Transposition - A **transposition** that is a **variant** of the **base text** word rather than the actual word. See pp. 23-24, 43-44.

Vorlage - The Hebrew text which underlies a manuscript or family of manuscripts. See also **archetype**.

Abbreviations

*	original, uncorrected writing of the first scribal hand
~ ~	the reading within the tildes is transposed by those manuscripts included
~~ ~	the same as the above, except that this time it is a virtual transposition
[ ]	the reading enclosed by the brackets is not supported by a majority of the family under study
ᵃ	the correction by the original hand or by a contemporary
ᵇ	the correction by a later hand
ˣ	it is not known which hand supplied the correction
?	the reading is unclear
>	becomes
<	derives from
ALQ²	Cross, *The Ancient Library of Qumran and Modern Studies,* revised edition, 1961
aor	aorist
B-M	*The Old Testament in Greek . . . ,* ed. Brooke, McLean and Thackeray
BHS	*Biblia Hebraica Stuttgartensia*
BIOSCS	*Bulletin of the International Organization for Septuagint and Cognate Studies*
CATSS	Computer Assisted Tools for Septuagint Studies
CE	Common Era
cf	*confer(endum)*: compare

decl	declension
fem	feminine
gr	Greek
hab	*habet*: it has
hex	hexaplaric
H-P	*Vetus Testamentum graecum cum variis lectionibus*, ed. Holmes and Parsons
HGTS	Ulrich, *The Hebrew and Greek Texts of Samuel*
HTR	*Harvard Theological Review*
IDB	*Interpreter's Dictionary of the Bible*
IDBS	*Interpreter's Dictionary of the Bible*, Supplementary Volume
impf	imperfect
JBL	*Journal of Biblical Literature*
JTS	*Journal of Theological Studies*
Kms	Kingdoms
Luc	Lucian/ic
LXX	Septuagint
maj	majority
masc	masculine
mg	margin; marginal gloss
mg¹	first of more than one marginal glosses
MS(S)	manuscript(s)
MT	Masoretic text
NT	New Testament
OG	Old Greek
OT	Old Testament
OTTV	Roberts, *The Old Testament Text and Versions*
p(p)	page(s)
pres	present
rell	*reliqui*: the rest
QHBT	*Qumran and the History of the Biblical Text*
Rgn	Reigns

Ruth	Abercrombie, et. al., *Computer Assisted Tools for Septuagint Studies.* Vol. 1, Ruth
SAJW	Thackeray, *The Septuagint and Jewish Worship*
Sam	Samuel
SAMS	Jellicoe, *The Septuagint and Modern Study*
SITS	Thackeray, *Studies in the Septuagint: Origins, Recensions, and Interpretations*, ed. Orlinsky
sub ※	under the hexaplaric asterisk
sub ÷	under the hexaplaric obelus
txt	text
vid	*videtur*: it seems
VTS	*Vetus Testamentum Supplement*

Introduction

In the past manuscripts boc_2e_2[1] have been studied principally for evidence of their Hebrew *Vorlage*. The present study concentrates on the text of the manuscripts themselves as it has been preserved, and focuses on the text of 1 Reigns.

Two previous works have been particularly important by way of background. Brock's unpublished Oxford dissertation "The Recensions of the Septuagint Version of I Samuel," and particularly the study of the Lucianic manuscripts in the second chapter which broke "entirely new ground,"[2] has proved foundational. Barthélemy's earlier *Les devanciers d'Aquila* has been motivational. In this important study he claimed that in Reigns the text of MSS boc_2e_2 is essentially the Old Greek, and that in the καίγε portion of 2 Reigns[3] they are the sole witness to the Old Greek tradition, the Old Greek having been replaced in all the other extant manuscripts of this section by the later "Palestinian" text. Because by its textual nature this hypothesis cannot be tested for 2 Reigns–if they are the sole witness to the Old Greek there is no external point of comparison to see whether this is true or not–the assessment is moved to 1 Reigns where the Old Greek has not been replaced by the later text.

---

[1] These are usually designated "Lucianic" as detailed below.

[2] Brock, "Recensions," p. x.

[3] This corresponds to Thackeray's βγ section. In this passage the Hebrew particle וגם is consistently translated by the (from the perspective of the rules of classical Greek) nonsense form καὶ γε or (as it has now been standardized,) καίγε.

1

There is, however, a third key ingredient: the computer. Research potential exists today that was scarcely dreamed of when Brock conducted his research, and it is upon this rich resource that this present study relies heavily to extend the study of MSS boc_2e_2 beyond his work.

Purpose

The purpose of this study of MSS boc_2e_2 in 1 Reigns is twofold: (1) to ascertain, by means of statistical analysis and comparison, the relationship between the Lucianic manuscripts boc_2e_2, and on the one hand the Old Greek as represented by MS B, and on the other hand the hexaplaric text as represented by MS A; and (2) to create profiles of the Lucianic variants by means of computer-based synoptic studies.

Limitations

Because of the broad range of possible subjects relevant to such a study it is necessary to limit the scope from the outset. First, the study is confined to the Greek texts. Important work is currently being done in translation technique with reference to the underlying Hebrew text, but such matters lie outside of, and, for the text of 1 Samuel, subsequent to this study.

Second, Lucianic studies have figured prominently and importantly in theories of the history of the text. A number of studies have been completed that point towards there being two separate strata in the Lucianic text for Reigns, one early, and one late.[4] Because the focus of

---

[4]Representative studies include: Cross, "The History of the Biblical Text in the Light of Discoveries in the Judaean Desert," *HTR* 57 (1964), 281-299; Brock, "Recensions," pp. 178-229; "*redivivus*," pp. 176-181; Shenkel, *Chronology*, pp. 5-21; Tov, "proto-Lucian," pp. 101-113; Ulrich, *Qumran*, pp. 15-37.

Tov, on the one hand, wrote "Like Cross, I propose that boc_2e_2 in the books of Reigns are composed of two layers. The second layer is the historical Lucian, and I suggest that its substratum contained either *the* Old Greek translation or any Old Greek translation (ibid, p. 103)." On the other hand, in the same article, he speaks with more exactness of three layers, subdividing the second one above: "... it is no easy task to define

this study is primarily on the final forms of the manuscripts as they exist today, and on reconstructing the text which underlies them irrespective of strata, it is essentially a synchronic study and in the main insensitive to diachronic considerations.[5]

Third, examples are not cited from outside of 1 Reigns. The other Books of Reigns are not cited because no comparable database was available for them, and hence no comparable precision of quotation. Examples are not cited from outside of Reigns because it is not known at this stage just how far the text-type represented by MSS boc_2e_2 in Reigns extended. Certainly the greater part of their text in the Octateuch does not share the same characteristics as it has in Samuel-Kings.[6] Was there ever a Lucianic recension for the whole of the Old Testament along the lines of that retained in Reigns? If there was, how much–if any–is extant in the available manuscripts? Metzger says:

---

criteria for unraveling the three layers of which boc_2e_2 are composed, viz. the Old Greek substratum, Lucian's borrowings from the "Three" and the fifth column of the Hexapla, and Lucian's own corrections" (ibid. p. 107).

In turn, Cross, as a prelude to his own triple strata concept, quoted Tov from the first quotation above as supporting only two layers, and ignored the second quotation where he speaks of three layers. Cross concludes: "There are in my view, however, three strata, not two, in the Lucianic text of Reigns. Tov's two strata analysis describes the Lucianic recension elsewhere in the Greek Bible where the *textus receptus* is the *Palestinian* text. The third or middle stratum in my view are [*sic*] corrections of the Old Greek to a Palestinian Hebrew text type in Reigns where *three* textual traditions exist, and where the *textus receptus* is *Non-palestinian*" ("Local Texts," p. 314; emphasis his).

In fact a total of four layers is being spoken of here, three of which Cross and Tov agree on: the Old Greek, the borrowings from the Hexapla, and the fourth century emendations. The fourth is the point of divergence between the two: that there is evidence of a distinct proto-Lucianic recension undertaken to bring the Old Greek in line with a Hebrew text that was still developing.

[5]The one exception to this is that portion of the statistical analysis in Chapter Two which compares MSS boc_2e_2 with MS B.

[6]Jellicoe says of Lagarde's attempted reconstruction of the Lucianic text: "Lagarde, unfortunately, had far overestimated the textual homogeneity of his manuscripts with the result that his Octateuch, except for the last dozen verses of Ruth, is not Lucianic at all" (*SAMS*, p. 7).

> Nor should the investigator imagine that it will be possible in every case to distinguish neatly ordered families of witnesses; in his search for the Lucianic text he must be prepared to acknowledge that for some of the books of the Old Testament it has left no recognizable trace among extant manuscripts.[7]

Similarly, Wevers comments:

> The Lucianic text can usually be identified from extensive biblical quotations found in Theodoret and Chrysostom. From these, in turn, certain MSS can be classified as Lucianic for certain books. E.g., it is clear that for the four books of the Kingdoms MSS b b' o r c_2 e_2 are clearly Lucianic, whereas manuscripts g i and H(olmes) P(arson) 246 have numerous Lucianic readings. Marginal Lucianic readings are to be found in the Syro-Hexaplar and in MSS M and j. It should be carefully noted, however, that this applies only to these books. For other LXX books the textual character is quite different.[8]

Although various lists of the characteristics of the Lucianic text exist, I do not believe it wise or prudent to accept this evidence at this stage, as tempting as that is, because the sources for the criteria are too widely drawn. Some–and only some–of the evidence is taken from MSS bo[r]$c_2$$e_2$ in Reigns,[9] especially in comparison with scriptural quotations

---

[7]Metzger, *Chapters*, p. 14.

[8]Wevers, "Septuagint," *IDB*, IV:276 (note that MS r is not extant for 1 Reigns). Of further interest is the following statement by him: "The Antiochian or Lucianic recension has been clearly identified in the Prophetic Canon; it is still problematic for the Pentateuch as a whole. There is some evidence of non-hexaplaric recensional activity influenced by the Hebrew text in the closely related groups which I have isolated as the d and t families; it is not impossible that these represent Lucian, though it remains an inexplicable fact that the quotations by Chrysostom and Theodoret do not represent this text" (*VTS* 29, p. 393).

[9]Shenkel (*op. cit.* p. 11), commenting on the early stratum in Lucian, says: "It is not possible at the present stage of Septuagint research to determine the extent of the proto-Lucianic recension for the whole of the OT text. However, because extensively preserved manuscripts of the Palestinian Hebrew text of the same type as the *Vorlage* of the proto-Lucian recension have been found at Qumran for both Books of Samuel, it is safe to conclude that the proto-Lucianic text form is present as the basic stratum in the Lucian text for the Books of Samuel and Kings." What is true of the early stratum is also true of the whole text.

by the Syrian Fathers such as Chrysostom, Theodoret and Theodore of
Mopsuestia; some is taken from Field's work in the Syro-Hexaplar;[10]
some is taken from the Syrian New Testament texts; and some is taken
from manuscripts which are perceived to be Lucianic, and described as
being "more or less Lucianic" depending upon the extent to which they
share these characteristics.[11] The problem is that the identification of
a text as Antiochian (or Syrian) through the scriptural citations in the
Syrian Fathers outside of Reigns does not in itself guarantee that the
manuscripts so identified share the same characteristics as MSS boc$_2$e$_2$ in
Reigns. Especially is this true when manuscripts from outside of Samuel-
Kings share some characteristics but have more besides which are then

---

[10]Cross, commenting on the situation with relation to what he calls "the proto-
Lucianic recension," says "In the past, the primary data for isolating the proto-Lucianic
recension derived from the βγ and γδ sections of Reigns. With the demonstration by
Barthélemy that in these sections the *kaige* Recension has replaced the Old Greek, most
of this evidence disappeared. Many readings formerly labeled proto-Lucianic are merely
Old Greek, the substratum of the Lucianic tradition preserved in boc$_2$e$_2$ ("Local Texts,"
p. 313).

[11]Swete, writing of the readings in the Syro-Hexaplar under the siglum λ that Field
identified as signifying Lucianic readings, says: "... the readings thus marked as Lucianic
occur also in the cursive Greek MSS. 19, 82, 93, 108; and further examination shewed that
these four MSS. in the Books of Kings, Chronicles, and Ezra-Nehemiah agree with the text
of the LXX. offered by the Antiochian fathers Chrysostom and Theodoret, who might
have been expected to cite from 'Lucian'. Similar reasoning led Field to regard codd. 22,
36, 48, 51, 62, 90, 93, 144, 147, 233, 308 as presenting a more or less Lucianic text in the
Prophets" (*Intro.*, p. 83).
    In commenting upon the work of Field, Metzger says: "Later scholars, however,
have criticized Field's grouping, and some of the manuscripts have been removed from
his list of Lucianic witnesses. Thus, Cornill struck out four (62, 90, 147, 233), and in this
he was supported by Lagarde. In the minor prophets, the doctoral research of a young
Dutch scholar, Schuurmans Stekhoven, indicated a slightly different grouping of
manuscripts .... He also pointed out that they do not all supply the Lucianic text in an
equally pure form" (*Chapters*, p. 9).

added to the list of Lucianic characteristics on the basis that they are "more or less Lucianic."[12]

Assumptions

From the results of previous work in Septuagintal studies in general and the Lucianic manuscripts in particular come six conclusions that relate directly to this present work, and combine to form important background material. These conclusions have not been restudied; rather they are assumed on the authority of the research and their general acceptance within the field.

The first assumption is that for 1 Reigns MS B is the best witness to, and lies close to, the Old Greek. Shenkel comments:

> The best witness in Samuel and Kings for the pre-hexaplaric text of the Old Greek is the Codex Vaticanus .... Fortunately, the purity of this codex as a witness to a pre-hexaplaric text seems to be greatest precisely in the Books of Samuel and Kings.[13]

There is wide support for this view, but it is not without dissension. Some have linked the codex with the name of Hesychius. Jellicoe was

---

[12]Outside of Reigns the adjectives 'Lucianic' (in the narrower sense of referring to the text-type contained in MSS boc₂e₂ in Reigns) and 'Syrian' or 'Antiochian' are not necessarily synonymous. A text may be 'Syrian' in that its provenance can be traced to Syria, without its being 'Lucianic' in the sense of sharing the characteristics of MSS boc₂e₂ in 1-4 Reigns. The clearest example is the text of these manuscripts in the Octateuch where it is agreed that they are not 'Lucianic' (until Ruth 4:11), but this does not mean that they are thereby not 'Syrian.' Failure to recognize this has caused unnecessary confusion.

[13]Shenkel, *Chronology*, p. 8. Driver concurs when he says: "That of all MSS. of LXX, B ... as a rule, exhibits relatively the purest and most original Septuagint text, is generally allowed" (*Notes*, p. xlvi).

associated with the revival of this link, one originally proposed by Grabe.[14] However, Brock concludes:

> ... in the textual tradition, as it comes down to us, of I Kms there is no evidence for definite recensional activity outside the work of Origen and 'Lucian', and so if Hesychius is to be connected with any text type of this book (and Bya₂Eth have the best, or rather, least unsatisfactory, claims), then the Hesychian ἔκδοσις must have been of the type envisaged in the preceding paragraphs [a reissue of an existing text], and not a recension proper.[15]

It is recognized that it is not possible to prove the link between MS B and the Old Greek. It is rather demonstrated by showing the absence of the later hexaplaric material. This in turn raises the question of whether the text of MS B may not in fact have been intentionally created by the systematic omission of readings from a hexaplaric manuscript. However, in more practical terms, it is reasonable to continue on the assumption that MS B bears a close and striking relationship to the Old Greek whether that is an original relation or one artificially contrived.[16]

The second assumption is that MSS Acx are the prime hexaplaric witnesses in 1 Reigns. Referring to Samuel-Kings, Wevers says:

> Though individually [MSS] Alex and x show peculiarities, they (together with the Armenian and Syro-Hexaplar) constitute the best evidence in these books for the Hexaplaric recension.[17]

---

[14]"The Hesychian Recension Reconsidered," *JBL*, vol. 82 (1963), pp. 409-418. In his Introduction, Jellicoe simply comments of the codex that "... from the time of Grabe onwards it has been widely identified with the recension of Hesychius" (*SAMS*, p. 177).

[15]"Recensions," p. 34.

[16]Brock notes of MS B and congeners that "they do indeed show a tendency towards abbreviation, but abbreviation as the outcome of scribal carelessness rather than conscious effort, and all the characteristics that go to identify these mss as a group are of this type" ("Recensions," pp. 33, 34).

[17]Wevers, "Proto-Septuagint," p. 59, n. 6. The reason that he does not mention MS c in this connection is because it is hexaplaric only for Samuel (see Shenkel, *Chronology*, p. 20). Johnson confirms this assessment: "Den hexaplarischen Text repräsentieren in

From this group MS A is selected for the statistical study in Chapter II.

The third, stemming historically from the connection made by Ceriani in 1861, and since then receiving much support, is that it is appropriate to refer to MSS boc$_2$e$_2$ as 'the Lucianic manuscripts.'[18] Brock has demonstrated that there is clear evidence of recensional work in the text represented by these manuscripts that is best dated around the fourth century CE, the time of the *floruit* of the traditional Lucian.[19]

1Sam hauptsächlich A cx (*Rezension*, p. 89).

[18]In Ceriani's day it was a case of a name looking for a text. Jerome said in his Preface to Chronicles: "*Constantinopolis usque Antiochiam Luciani martyris exemplaria probat.*" This provided the name, it remained simply to find the text that bore the closest accord with the text cited by the Syrian Fathers. For further detail see: Ulrich, *Qumran*, pp. 15-18.

A similar phenomenon is to be seen in the various (unsuccessful) attempts to find a text to which the name of Hesychius can be attached.

[19]Brock concludes: "What then, if anything, did Lucian have to do with the text to be found in *L*[ucian]? The relevant facts are basically as follows: on the one side, on Jerome's specific statement, supported by all later tradition, Lucian undertook a revision of the Biblical text. On the other side we are presented with a distinctive text which achieved the form we now know by the first half of the fourth century, when it was current around Antioch. The *terminus post quem* for this final formulation, it is important to remember, is not known. This distinctive Antiochene text is quite definitely largely (but *not* wholly) the result of recensional activity, though whether all the recensional features go back to the same hand is far from certain: some non-hexaplaric approximations, at least, appear to go back to a fairly early stratum. But the grammatical and stylistic improvements seem, on the admittedly rather scanty evidence available, to be contemporary with, or later than, the introduction of hexaplaric material.

"Thus it can be said that two of the features most characteristic of the text of *L* do appear to fall within Lucian's lifetime. This being so, it seems justifiable to retain the traditional designation of the Antiochene text as Lucianic: if Lucian himself did not put it into its final form, it was a close contemporary of his who did" ("Recensions," pp. 307, 308).

Jellicoe is representative of those who use the term while retaining reservations when he says: "The putative author of the Lucianic recension ..." (*SAMS*, p. 157). Tsevat, in a parenthetic comment on the use of the word 'Lucianic,' says it "... serves here as a conventional appellation comparable to 'Septuaginta,' Seventy [Translators]" ("Samuel I, II," *IDBS*, 778). However, in the light of Brock's research (and the research of those before him) the appellation does indicate provenance–Syria(=Antioch), and time (the *floruit* of the traditional Lucian), even though the identification with the martyr Lucian himself will never be absolutely certain.

Barthélemy, in the paragraph headed provocatively "La prétendue 'recension lucianique,'" proposed that scholarship no longer speak of a Lucianic text or recension,[20] although he did recognize the existence of an Antiochian text for some books, including Reigns,[21] which had undergone hexaplaric contamination.[22] While Brock and Barthélemy are by no means in agreement on this point they are not as far apart as would at first appear: they both recognize that the text is distinctive, that its provenance is Syria, that it contains early and late strata–with much of the later material coming from the hexapla, but much of the earlier material being significant for preserving important readings[23]. What is perhaps most damaging to Barthélemy's position is the fact, pointed out by Ulrich, that the text of MSS boc_2e_2 meets the criteria that Barthélemy himself laid down for constituting a recension.[24]

In the light of all of this it is appropriate to continue the use of the terms Lucian and Lucianic in relation to MSS boc_2e_2 in Reigns.

The fourth is that these Lucianic manuscripts form a homogeneous group or family. The following table sets out their details:[25]

---

[20]"Je propose donc que l'on renonce à ces désignations dans la critique textuelle de la Septante, même si certains glossateurs de manuscrits grecs et syriaques les ont employées" (*Devanciers*, p. 127).

[21]"Pour certains livres (et c'est le cas pour les Règnes) on pourra parler de „text antiochien" dans la mesure où cette forme textuelle est assez caractérisée et où son usage par l'école d'Antioche est assez bien établi. Mais ne considérons pas ce „text antiochien" comme le fruit d'une recension autonome ou, pour employer le language ancien, comme constituant une „édition" spéciale" (ibid.).

[22]"L'originalité et l'intérêt du „text antiochien" ne consistera donc pas pour nous dans les recensions qu'il a subies, car elles dépendent essentiellement des hexaples" (ibid.).

[23]"Cette originalité et cet intérêt consisteront au contraire dans les importants éléments de la Septante ancienne qu'il nous a seul conservés" (ibid.).

[24]Ulrich, *Qumran*, pp. 31, 32.

[25]The table is based on that of Ulrich (*Qumran*, p. 21), with some reordering.

Table 1

B-M	H-P	Lagarde	Century	Library
b′	19	h	xi-xii	Rome, Chigi, R. vi. 38
b	108	d	xiii-xiv	Rome, Vat. Gr. 330
o	82	f	xii-xiii	Paris, Bibl. Nat., Coisl. 3
c₂	127		x	Moscow, Syn. Libr. Gr. 31
e₂	93	m	xiii-xiv	London, Br. Mus. Royal I. D. II[26]

Though these five manuscripts are now recognized as forming a group in 1 Reigns, it was not until 1904 that Rahlfs added MS c₂, hence the lack of a Lagarde letter in the table above. This is surprising to the modern scholar accustomed to seeing them as a group in the apparatus of B-M. However, when H-P was the only source for the listing of variants, the data for MS 127 [c₂] was not included in the body of the text but was listed separately in the "Addenda et Emendanda" where it was more difficult to recognize the now obvious connection.

Brock's assessment is:

> The group as a whole is remarkably unified. c₂, however, provides rather more hexaplaric matter (sometimes also with the signs) than do the other four mss. As in III-IV Kms [Rahlfs, *LXX Studien I*, p. 5] the *Vorlage* of o must have had some lacunae in this book too: thus [in] xxx 30 - xxxi 11 o ceases to be Lucianic, having filled up a lacuna with a text of non-Lucianic type.[27]

In addition, he says of their text in 1 Reigns in contrast to 3-4 Reigns: "It should be noted that in the last two books of Kms there is

---

[26]The dates are on the authority of Ulrich. Swete (*Intro.* pp. 148-152) lists them (in the same order as the table) as: ?x, xiv, xii, x, xiii; and Jellicoe (*SAMS*, p. 163), who updated Swete, concurs.

The two MSS b′ and b are closely related, and unless they have separate readings they are listed simply as b (as per B-M).

[27]Brock, "Recensions," p. 17. Busto Saiz says "In our opinion this appraisal can be detailed with more precision reducing it to 1 King[dom]s 31,3-10. Moreover, manuscript 82 [o] has the same textual type in 2 King[dom]s 1,19-2,2" ("On the Lucian Manuscripts in 1-2 Kings," pp. 305-306).

often quite a sharp division between bc$_2$ and oe$_2$, which is rarely apparent in the earlier books."[28]

The fifth accepts the groupings of the non-Lucianic manuscripts in 1 Reigns which have been established by previous scholars.[29] Brock provides the following list:[30]

> Bya$_2$ - This group is generally considered to be the best witness to the original Old Greek text of 1 Kms.
>
> Acx - This is the chief hexaplaric group, but the inner relationship is by no means always close, nor do the members always have hexaplaric readings together.
>
> dlpqtz - Next to [Acx] this group is the best hexaplaric witness, but only as far as xxi .... Basically the text is fairly close to MN+.
>
> efmsw - This group, of which e is not a very consistent member, is otherwise fairly well defined.
>
> MNaghijnvb$_2$ - This is an amorphous and characterless group.

The final assumed result of earlier scholarship is that there was an original text of 1 Reigns and that it was the work of one translator. In this connection the conclusion of Brock is accepted:

> As far as I Kms is concerned, the matter in common between L[ucian] and LXX *rell* is so great that it would have required a Philonic miracle (and then not a very competent one, in view of the actual divergences) to have brought about such a close identity of two different translations. Consequently it may be safely assumed that our Greek text of I Kms goes back to a single translation: if there did ever exist another one, or other ones, the only traces they can be supposed to have left will

---

[28]Brock, "Recensions," p. 195.

[29]L. Dieu, "Les manuscripts grecs des Livres de Samuel," *Le Muséon* 24 (1921), pp. 17-60; Rahlfs, *Septuaginta-Studien* I, p. 502; Johnson, *Rezension*, pp. 19, 20.

[30]Brock, "Recensions," pp. 12-19. The summaries are from his descriptions. Non-greek texts are not listed here.

be in individual passages or variants where they have contaminated the surviving translation (or manuscripts of this).[31]

Method and outline

Before detailing the approach and outline it will be helpful to view the overall method which has two stages, the latter building on and moving logically beyond the former.

The first stage is the analysis of two statistical profiles collated against MS B (representing the Old Greek) and MS A (representing the hexaplaric material) in 1 Reigns. The minority readings of the collation manuscripts were first selected from the database, adjusted as necessary as detailed in Chapter Two, and then tabulated for the two families–Bya$_2$ and Acx–and the Lucianic manuscripts. Finally the results were studied to ascertain the relationships of the manuscripts and families to the collation manuscripts and to each other.

The second stage is the analysis of the Lucianic variants. To focus the study, the material included in the analysis is limited to the distinctive Lucianic variants according to guidelines detailed in Chapter Three. Then these variants are studied to ascertain the characteristics and discernible trends of the Lucianic text.

The Outline of the Chapters then is as follows: Chapter I details the creation of the computer database: its layout, adaptations, standardization, and terminology.

Chapter II is a comparative statistical analysis of three selected families of manuscripts: Vaticanus (Bya$_2$), Alexandrinus (Acx) and the

---

[31]Brock, "Recensions," p. 31. Barthélemy similarly says of what he terms the Palestinian and Antiochian texts: "Il existe donc à la base de ces deux traditions *une* Septante ancienne" ("Reexamination," pp. 28, 30). Wevers says: "There is to my mind no doubt that the Antiochian text was an early revision of the Septuagint text. That it was a revision rather than a separate translation can be demonstrated from a careful study of the Lucianic text. No two separate translations could have made the same peculiar mistranslations in so many places" ("Proto-Septuagint," p. 69).

Lucianic manuscripts (boc_2e_2). The first analysis is a collation of the families in relationship to MS B, the second in relationship to MS A. These collations are done to establish the relationship of the Lucianic text to both the Old Greek and the hexaplaric material.

Chapters III and IV contain the analysis of the Lucianic variants. First the readings supported by a majority of the Lucianic manuscripts are studied, followed by the analysis of those supported by a minority of the Lucianic manuscripts. For convenience each set of variants–those supported by a majority of the Lucianic manuscripts, and those supported by a minority of the Lucianic manuscripts–is divided according to where its variants occur among the five database categories: base text, omissions, substitutions, transpositions, and additions. Further, in each of these five categories those variants that consist of two or more words are studied independently of the single word variants. From this is obtained a list of the identifiable characteristics of the Lucianic manuscripts and the profiles of the types of variants that occur.

The Conclusion contains a summary of the results of the study.

Texts and Editions

The base text for the database is the Rahlfs text that was put into machine-readable form by the *Thesaurus Linguae Graecae* project and made available under the auspices of CATSS. Around this text were grouped the variants of the Greek manuscripts listed in the second apparatus of B-M which were manually entered and accented, etc. In those places in Chapters 17 and 18 where MS B and congeners do not have the longer text of the MT tradition,[32] the text of MS A from the B-M apparatus was used instead, and the variants of the other (hexaplaric) manuscripts grouped around this text.

---

[32]17:12-31, 41, 50, 55-58; 18:1-5, 10, 11, 17-19, 30.

All, and only, the Greek material of the second apparatus was included.[33] Where there was any uncertainty about readings manual comparison was made to the Lagarde text[34] and H-P.[35] This material includes the quotations from the Greek Church Fathers as well as several manuscripts listed solely on the basis of H-P.[36] Because of the fragmentary nature of the quotations and the H-P material–as a general rule the B-M apparatus shows where they have a reading, not where they do not–they are not included in the statistical analysis.

B-M list the following as having lacunae in 1 Reigns:[37]

A	12:18-14:9
M	4:19-10:19; 14:26-25:33
g	13:9-14:43
h	6:13-7:1; 13:3-14:1; 22:9-24:17
j	1:1-14:49
l	1:1-14:32; 30:15-31:13
m	6:10-10:25
v	2:1-10

---

[33]The first apparatus contains orthographic variants from the major uncials (chiefly MS B), while the third apparatus contains readings from other Greek translations ("the three," etc.) gleaned from the various hexaplaric witnesses.

[34]Although the Lagarde text does not *per se* form a part of this study, it was useful as a point of reference. It was manually compared with the majority text for the thirty-one chapters of 1 Reigns to ascertain which of the Lucianic texts formed the basis of Lagarde's text, and to discover what principles guided him in his selection of readings.

[35]Ulrich characterizes this work as "... the praiseworthy but not altogether trustworthy edition ... (*Qumran*, p. 19)." Certainly it could not be relied upon for the creation of the database, but it has proved invaluable for reference checking.

[36]All of the last material is enclosed in angle brackets in the database in accord with the B-M practice to distinguish it from the rest of the material thus: "<246>".

[37]These are physical lacunae from damaged manuscripts as opposed to textual omissions. In addition, MSS By Nanvb₂ do not have the hexaplaric material in chapters 17 and 18, where they witness to a shorter text. Other manuscripts also lack one or more parts–but not all–of this material.

CHAPTER I

Creation of the Database

In this chapter the creation of the computer database is detailed: its layout, adaptations, standardization, and terminology.

The Database

When this study began there was no database available for 1 Reigns, so the first step was to enter manually[1] all the variants from B-M on a microcomputer.[2] The format was fundamentally according to the CATSS specifications.[3] The Rahlfs text was used as the base text,[4] and

---

[1]This method is no longer necessary with the availability of the Kurzweil Data Entry Machine which can 'read' the variants from the page and automatically encode the information ready for reformatting and verification by a series of computer programs. At the final stage line-by-line verification (and sometimes modification) is necessary.

[2]The computer available at the time of data entry (1983) was an eight bit CP/M business machine with 64K of RAM and an 11 megabyte hard disk. Due to these memory limitations fixed length fields were not possible which necessitated more of a wordprocessing than a dataprocessing approach, and smaller programming steps.

[3]For a full description of these specifications, see *Ruth*, pp. 53-68; and *BIOSCS* 14:22-40. In 1 Reigns there were times when there were more than 99 items in a verse, so it was necessary to increase the number of digits in the item count (the "02" in the first line of the example below) from two to three digits (the "001" in the second line). With the extra digit there were now five digits together, and while this is no problem for a computer, it was difficult for the eye to read, especially as the two sets of numbers increment independently, so a space was inserted between them. As a consequence the start of text is not in the same column for Reigns as it is for Ruth. When books like Psalms that have more than 99 chapters and/or more than 99 verses are entered into the

15

the Greek variant data, including the Greek Patristic citations,[5] were

---

database the columns will be moved again. The following comparisons between Ruth ("RT") and 1 Reigns ("1R") illustrate this:

RT 03 05(0200) + <και 18
1R 01 01(001 00) + <και Abcoxya2c2e2 Eus

RT 03 05(0200) ειπεν
1R 01 01(003 01) ανθρωπος] > ~b´ Chr~

While this is only a minor programming irritation, it does indicate that the format used in Ruth will not be the final standard, and will have to be adjusted upwards to accommodate the larger biblical Books. See further Taylor: "The CATSS Variant Database: An Evaluation" (*BIOSCS* 25 [1992]).

⁴This was available through CATSS, having been encoded by *Thesaurus Linguae Graecae*. For an explanation of the choice of the Rahlfs text for the base text see *Ruth*, pp. 9, 10. In this database, where the Rahlfs text–compared to the Hebrew text–lacks verses, the lacunae are supplied from other manuscripts–principally MS A–and were taken from the text which heads the entry for each of these verses in the apparatus of B-M (see p. 13, f.n. 32), This fact is not noted in the database except as it is recorded for extended passages that MS B and congeners lack the base text material supplied from MS A.

⁵The variants from versions derived from the Greek were not included at this time to conserve computer disk space and program time, inasmuch as they were not directly germane to this study. This decision was necessary to remain within the capabilities of the system and the time available, and leaves this material to be entered and researched at a later date. The flexibility of the format readily permits the addition of such data even in different languages.

One area needing full investigation, especially in Reigns, is the relation of the Old Latin to the Lucianic text. A preliminary investigation conducted in the first eight chapters of 1 Reigns that compared the Greek, the Old Latin (from B-M and *BHS*) and the Hebrew, indicated a promising, even if complex, area of research.

In this connection see Ulrich's article (and bibliography) on the Old Latin, particularly in its relationship to Samuel, "The Old Latin Translation of the LXX and the Hebrew Scrolls from Qumran" (Emanuel Tov, ed, *HGTS*, pp. 121-165). While he recognizes that "large-scale hypotheses or conclusions would be premature," he nevertheless notes that: "[Old] L[atin] proves to be a reasonably faithful and controllable witness to the Old Greek, which in turn is not infrequently a witness superior to the Massoretic text for the ancient text of Samuel" (ibid., p. 156).

This is in some contrast to Brock who earlier had concluded: "Because of the incomplete and unsatisfactory nature of the evidence available it would be pointless to try to use [the Old] Lat[in] as a guide to 'pre-Lucianic' in *L*[ucian]. This is not, of course,

entered from the B-M apparatus using the standard format.[6] The Rahlfs text included accents and breathing marks, but the material from the apparatus lacked them as did the base text readings taken from the B-M apparatus which were used to supply the verses lacking in the Rahlfs text.[7] These marks were added manually to enable accurate searches now and to be available later for morphological analysis by CATSS.[8]

Adaptations

The information from the B-M apparatus had to be adapted to conform to the database format in two recurring situations. The first

---

to deny that variants witnessed by the combination *L* Lat *may* not sometimes, or indeed often, be 'pre-Lucianic': there are simply no means of judging .... Nor again is this to deny the value of Lat for purposes of textual criticism: Lat is the repository of a great many elements of very diverse origin; some of these are valuable, some are not, but it is only possible to judge which are valuable on purely internal grounds" ("Recensions," p. 222).

In connection with Lucianic studies Tov concludes "I should like to emphasize once again the importance of the Vetus Latina and other pre-Lucianic sources in pinpointing the ancient elements of boc_2e_2" ("Proto-Lucian," p. 108).

[6]The listings of the manuscripts (in the database, but not in the critical text) retain the alphabetical order used by B-M with the uncials first followed by the minuscules (which also happens to be computer ASCII order) except that the priority given by B-M to MS B amongst the uncials (as in "BAMN") is eliminated. Where there is more than one grouping of manuscripts for a variant these are also in the same alphabetic (or ASCII) order by the first letter of each group. All patristic material is listed after the B-M material, and the H-P manuscripts are listed last.

Wherever possible, to conserve space, B-M abbreviated the listings using spans, citing only the first and last letter of a continuous series separated by a dash as in 'a-f' for 'abcdef'. All of these were expanded to full listings during data entry to assist in programming. The division of the listings into families such as "boc_2e_2," "dlpqtz" for the critical text was performed later by software.

[7]See p. 13, f.n. 32.

[8]Due to data transfer difficulties it was not possible to utilize the morphological feature of CATSS fully (see *Ruth*, pp. 69-84). A printout of the raw analysis of the Rahlfs text was available and was useful as far as it went, but beyond that the work was done manually.

adaptation concerns spans with multiple readings,[9] and multiple plusses longer than a few words. They are essentially the same, except that the first occurs where there are variations to the order of the base text, and the second occurs where there are multiple additions to the base text.

Both of them can be handled in one of two ways: in the case of the span with multiple readings one can either use omission signs with corresponding plusses,[10] or integrate the variants into the base text using

---

[9]In this context a span is a lemma longer than two words cited by using only the first and last words separated by a dash. Many of the spans have only one variant reading such as the omission of the lemma passage and are readily adapted to the database format. The situation of interest here is when there are multiple variant readings to such a lemma passage. At 1:5 there is:

την–ελκανα] ηγαπα ο ελκανα την ανναν boe$_2$: ελκανα ηγαπα την ανναν c$_2$.

In some situations that were too complex to be handled in this way B-M used another alternative. The critical apparatus first of all has a representative text consisting of the majority readings from the manuscripts that share the passage, and then the variants follow one by one in the usual way, but this whole block of variants is marked off by double square brackets to indicate that they are a subset of the combined reading thus: "[[. . . . .]]" (e.g. B-M, p. 94, 27:8).

[10]The example from 1:5 cited above would appear as follows:

$$την] \ > \ \sim boc_2e_2\sim$$
$$Αvvαv] \ > \ \sim boc_2e_2\sim$$
$$ηγαπα] \ > \ \sim boc_2e_2\sim$$
$$Eλκανα] \ > \ \sim boc_2e_2\sim$$
$$+ \ ηγαπα \ boe_2$$
$$+ \ o \ boe_2$$
$$+ \ ελκανα \ boe_2$$
$$+ \ την \ boe_2$$
$$+ \ ανναν \ boe_2$$
$$+ \ ελκανα \ c_2$$
$$+ \ ηγαπα \ c_2$$
$$+ \ την \ c_2$$
$$+ \ ανναν \ c_2.$$

In this case there is no integration at all.

plusses and omissions only where strictly necessary.[11] Similarly, in the case of the multiple plusses, either each of the units is listed separately one after the other in the database, or they are integrated into one unified master reading along with the variants to it.[12]

The advantage of the former method is that when the database is edited back into a critical text the integrity of each individual unit can be maintained. The advantage of the latter method is that the database is highly integrated. The disadvantage of each method is the converse of the advantage of the other. While the former easily converts back to the individual units it is not integrated; because the latter is integrated it does not easily convert back to the individual units.

In this database it was decided to sacrifice the ease of conversion in favor of an integrated text.[13] Consequently, when the majority text

---

[11]The same example appears in the database thus:

$$την] > \sim boc_2e_2\sim$$
$$Avvαν] > \sim boc_2e_2\sim$$
$$ηγαπα] > \sim c_2\sim$$
$$+ o\ boe_2$$
$$Ελκανα$$
$$+ ηγαπα \sim c_2\sim$$
$$+ την \sim boc_2e_2\sim$$
$$+ αvvαv \sim boc_2e_2\sim$$

In this case the readings are fully integrated.

[12]There is an example at 1:6. Here there are three extended "pr" passages ranging in length from nine to nineteen words (see B-M, p. 2). Even though all of these passages have much in common with each other B-M made no effort to integrate them, preferring to list them separately. In the database one could have followed their lead and simply cited each of the readings separately, one after the other. However if this had been done it would have hidden the fact that they have much in common. Rather it was preferred to combine the three readings into one unified master reading along with the variants to it (see Vol. I, p. 2 of this study).

[13]This then is similar to the third method of B-M described above where they used an integrated text and a block of variants as a subset within the apparatus marked off by double square brackets. Had they done this for spans as well then virtually all of the apparatus would have been integrated.

in Volume I was created, the Lucianic readings were often subdivided into smaller units by the computer program because of uneven support from non-Lucianic manuscripts. By manually editing the text it was possible to restore the integrity of the longer Lucianic variants.[14]

The second adaptation involves the "rell" readings.[15] They are used by B-M in conjunction with lemma readings of MS B supported by a minority of all the manuscripts.[16] First, the lemma reading with its

---

[14]This was done in one of two ways. Where the variants were closely similar to the Lucianic reading the differences were listed either in the text of the reading or after the particular manuscript concerned, to restore the longer readings. This is illustrated from the passage in 1:6 already noted above:

καιγε … δια το εξουθενειν (εξουδενουσα c_2) αυτην boc_2(> καιγε-το) g(> καιγε-εξουθενειν)h Chr(vid)

Where the variant readings were substantially different, especially in length, only the longer Lucianic variants were retained. An example from 4:4 illustrates this. The database reads:

+ των Abdopqtzc$_2$e$_2$
+ δυναμεων Abdopqtzc$_2$e$_2$
+ ου boc$_2$e$_2$ z$^{a?}$
+ επεκαθητο boc$_2$e$_2$ z$^{a?}$

Rather than retain the two separate units generated by the program (των δυναμεων boc$_2$e$_2$ A dpqtz, ου επεκαθητο boc$_2$e$_2$ z$^{a?}$) the reading in the critical text is simply:

των δυναμεων ου επεκαθητο boc$_2$e$_2$ z$^{a?}$.

[15]This abbreviation stands for *reliqui*: "the rest." At 21:15 (Rahlfs 21:16) B-M have the following reading, cited without the non-Greek witnesses:

ελαττουμαι Bx] pr ει a$_2$: pr μη eflmsw: η προσδεομαι b(hab ελαττομε b^{ms})oz$^{a?}$c$_2$e$_2$: pr η ANz* rell

In this case 'rell' stands for MSS dghijnpqtvyb$_2$.

[16]When the majority reading is the lemma (the usual situation), only the variants are listed. In this case the lemma is an implied "rell" and is to be understood as such in this discussion. When the lemma is a minority reading (as in the example above from 21:15) the readings of all of the other manuscripts have to be listed, otherwise it would be assumed that those not listed shared the reading of the lemma.

support–MS B and any other manuscripts–is cited; second, any other minority readings are listed; and finally the majority reading (or where it is not a majority reading, the last reading) is listed, with any uncials cited first, and then the abbreviation "rell" to indicate that the rest of the cursives not already cited share this reading.[17] By using this abbreviation B-M were able to save a great deal of space in the apparatus. In the database all of these "rell" listings are expanded to include the full list of the manuscripts covered by the "rell." To do this accurately it is necessary to exclude from the expanded list any manuscripts that omit (or transpose), or that substitute another reading, as well as to exclude any manuscripts that have a lacuna at this point.

Even so, in some instances, it is not possible to reconstruct accurately all of the information. Readings from the hand of the original scribe, where there are also corrections, are indicated by the addition of an asterisk (*) to the siglum for that particular manuscript, as in "b*."[18] When either the lemma or one of the minority readings contains an asterisked reading in conjunction with a "rell" reading, and B-M do not list the corrected reading as a separate minority reading, it is not possible to know which hand is the source of the corrected reading. All that is known is that it is either an *a* or a *b* reading, but not which one. Where B-M were not sure, they indicated their uncertainty by the use of the question mark thus: "b*?." To point up those situations where there is no

---

[17]The use of "rell" by B-M is specifically confined to the cursive manuscripts. As noted, if there are uncials that share the reading they are listed first; if there is support from the rest of the sources–the H-P manuscripts, the patristic sources or the non-greek manuscripts–they are listed individually after "rell."

[18]B-M say concerning the use of the asterisk: "The index * everywhere denotes the original writing of the scribe; and for MSS. other than BADEFS [where it carries a different significance] *a* denotes corrections by the same or an approximately contemporary hand, *b* corrections by a later hand" (*Genesis*, p. v).

certainty possible as to which hand was intended, the readings in the
critical text have been arbitrarily marked with an "x" as in "b^x."[19]

Standardization

A standardizing feature was added in accord with the practice of
both the Rahlfs and the Göttingen texts: the diphthong ει was standard-
ized to ι for proper names. Thus, instead of the two forms Δαυειδ and
Δαυιδ that occur in B-M, the reading is uniformly the latter. This had
only to be done for the variants, because it was already part of the Rahlfs
text used for the base text.

Database categories

Because of the layout of the data adopted by CATSS, readings are
found in one of five categories: base text, omissions, substitutions, trans-
positions, or additions.[20] Inasmuch as they are used both in the statis-

---

[19]See for example Vol. I, p. 39, 12:21: ουθεν Ac^{x}x.

[20]Below is a portion of the database from 1 Reigns 2 which contains readings for
all five categories:

1R 02 16(001 01) και] > A	[base text, omission]
1R 02 16(002 01) ελεγεν] > A	
.	
.	
1R 02 16(009 01) πρωτον] > ~i~	[base text, transposition]
1R 02 16(009 02) : προτερον boc₂e₂	[substitution]
1R 02 16(010 01) ως] > ~boc₂e₂~	
1R 02 16(011 01) καθηκει] > ~boc₂e₂~	
1R 02 16(012 00) + πρωτον ~i~	[transposition]
1R 02 16(013 00) το	
1R 02 16(014 00) στεαρ	
1R 02 16(015 00) + ως ~boc₂e₂~	[transposition]
1R 02 16(016 00) + καθηκει ~boc₂e₂~	
1R 02 16(017 00) και	
1R 02 16(018 00) + τοτε Nbfmosvwzc₂e₂	[addition]

tical analysis and the study of the Lucianic variants the categories are analyzed below.

1. Base text

The Rahlfs text is considered to be the "base text" except for the special cases listed below. This text is principally based on MS B with next priority going to MS A, and between them these two manuscripts account for most of the readings in the Rahlfs text. Because of this there is an apparent high degree of affinity between these two manuscripts in this category that is not reflected in any of the other categories.

Where the Rahlfs text does not include an extended passage that is present in the Hebrew text and is attested by some Greek manuscripts, other texts are used.[21] In the case of the hexaplaric material in chapters 17-18 the text is that of MS A, while at 13:1 (which is part of the lacuna of MS A) and 23:12 it is a composite text reconstructed from a number of manuscripts.

2. Omissions

This category records the manuscripts that do not share the reading of the base text. A manuscript may lack readings for a number of reasons such as: physical lacunae, haplography or similar copying oversights, a different text-type that does not accommodate readily to the base text, transpositions, and intentional omission of the base text reading by an editor as part of his redaction.

The base text reading and the manuscripts that omit it (if any) are on the same line, whereas substitutions, transpositions and additions each have their own line. These three are distinguished first from the base text by being indented one space, and from each other by their symbols: " : " for substitutions and " + " for transpositions and additions, except that where there are variants to the transpositions or additions the first symbol is " +:" and the subsequent symbols are " :+". Transpositions are distinguished from additions by the presence of the tildes surrounding the list of manuscripts that transpose.

[21]'Texts' rather than 'manuscripts' because in every instance these base text readings not supported by Rahlfs come from the texts in the apparatus of B-M that head each of these verses.

The only distinction between these different types of omissions in the database is that for transpositions. In this case the lists of manuscripts that transpose are surrounded by tildes. However if the transposition also includes a substitutional variant to the base text reading–what can be termed a 'virtual transposition'–it is not at present distinguished in the omission readings as a transposition, and appears both as an omission and as an addition, even though neither of these entries separately–nor both combined–adequately describe the situation.[22]

---

[22]The following extract contains an example of a virtual transposition: του ρηματος for το ρημα.

    1R 21 03(017 00) και
    1R 21 03(018 00) ειπεν
    1R 21 03(019 00) + προς Nabghijnovb₂c₂e₂
    1R 21 03(020 01) μοι] > cefmswx
    1R 21 03(020 02) : με Nabghijnovb₂c₂e₂
    1R 21 03(021 00) + μη Acdlpqtxz Or-gr
    1R 21 03(022 01) Μηδεις] > ~Acdlpqtxz Or-gr~
    1R 21 03(022 02) : μηθεις y
    1R 21 03(023 01) γνωτω]
    1R 21 03(023 02) : γνω aefgimsw
    1R 21 03(024 01) +:μηδεις ~Acdlpqtxz Or-gr~
    1R 21 03(024 02) :+μηδεν boc₂e₂
    1R 21 03(025 01) το] > ~~boc₂e₂~
    1R 21 03(026 01) ρημα] > ~~boc₂e₂~
    1R 21 03(027 00) + τουτο efimsw
    1R 21 03(028 00) περι
    1R 21 03(029 00) + του ~~boc₂e₂~
    1R 21 03(030 00) + ρηματος ~~boc₂e₂~
    1R 21 03(031 01) ου] > n*

Note that μηδεν is not a virtual transposition for the Lucianic manuscripts inasmuch as they have both this word and the preceding μηδεις, rather than the transposition which Acdlpqtxz Or-gr have.

    It would be helpful if virtual transpositions were brought under the present transposition symbol–the tilde. One way to achieve this would be to begin the virtual transposition entry with double tildes as shown above to distinguish it from the regular transposition. The database for this study does not contain any such marks because the problem was not identified until after the database was completed.

The physical layout of the database can easily be misunderstood to imply that manuscripts listed as omitting the base text words originally had these words but that they were not retained. While this is certainly possible it is not thereby to be assumed, and the converse is also possible: that the base text words were never part of the tradition of the "omitting" manuscripts, rather the words of the longer text (here the base text) were added to the tradition of the shorter text (as represented by the omission), a relation not visually portrayed by the current layout.[23]

In addition to the fact that the omission statistics are contaminated by the virtual transpositions there is the further problem of the relevance of omission statistics which is strikingly similar to the traditional *argumentum ex silentio*. Two (or more) manuscripts sharing the same reading is one thing, but two (or more) manuscripts omitting a particular reading is quite a different matter because there is no way to know from the database whether they omit because of a genetic relationship or simply by coincidence. Because so many disparate elements may be present in this category it is not possible to combine omission statistics with those of other categories in any meaningful way.

3. Substitutions

In this category the witness is to readings variant to the base text rather than to readings longer or shorter than the base text or in a different order. At the time of data entry a conscious effort was made to ensure that wherever possible parts of speech only substitute for others of the same type: nouns for nouns, verbs for verbs, etc.

4. Transpositions

At present this category is only used to record those places where manuscripts have the same words as the base text but in a different

---

[23]There is also a third possibility, that neither of the two traditions–that represented by the base text, and that represented by the omission(s)–bears any direct relation to the other.

order. Transpositions can be recorded in the database in more than one
way. Consider the following:

και ειπεν αυτω Δαυιδ
και ειπεν Δαυιδ αυτω

This can be represented in two ways:

και
ειπεν
αυτω] > ~boc₂e₂~
Δαυιδ
 + αυτω ~boc₂e₂~

και
ειπεν
 + Δαυιδ ~boc₂e₂~
αυτω
Δαυιδ] > ~boc₂e₂~

Relative to the base text, in the first case it is αυτω which is the trans-
position, while in the second it is Δαυιδ. While both convey the same
information, the former layout was preferred for this database with trans-
positions appearing first in their base text order (with the manuscript(s)
marked by tildes at the omission position) and then later in the trans-
posed position (with the manuscript(s) again marked by tildes). This is
more logical and convenient for analysis than forward references to a
base text word that has not yet appeared.[24]

       The consequence of this preference for transpositions following
their appearance in the base text is that the transposition markers in the
database only indicate a difference in word order rather than which word
or words were actually transposed by the original redactor. In the
example above it is not possible to know whether Δαυιδ or αυτω was
the word actually transposed. As a result tables of the parts of speech
transposed cannot be constructed in any meaningful way for this category.

---

[24]As more words are included in the transposition unit the number of layout options
correspondingly increase.

5. *Additions*

This category primarily records the readings of those manuscripts that have a text longer than the base text, although readings are also found here for other reasons. It was noted above that at present virtual transpositions are not included in transpositions so in addition to being listed under omission they are also found here.[25] Beyond these there are some readings that are included here because they could not be accommodated in any of the other categories due to fundamental differences in the texts. For instance when one word of the base text is replaced by two or more words, only one of them can be a substitution, and the rest are marked as additions.[26]

It can be seen from this analysis of the categories that the position of the readings within the five categories is determined by the base text, and that there are complementary relationships between categories. They are as follows: base text and substitutions, base text and transpositions, and omissions and additions. Thus the position of variants from a particular manuscript or family of manuscripts within the database is determined by the base text and that manuscript's relationship to the base text.

---

[25]For the analysis in Chapter Three the virtual transpositions were manually removed from both omissions and additions and included in the transpositions.

[26]Consider the following example:

καὶ
ειπεν
  + προς boc₂e₂
αυτω]
  : αυτον boc₂e₂
Δαυιδ

Both texts have the same meaning, but because boc₂e₂ have a longer text it is necessary to mark προς as an addition to accommodate to the format. For further details see *Ruth*, pp. 60-63.

Conclusion

The adaptation of the B-M apparatus to the CATSS database format provides a level of accuracy, accessibility, and flexibility commensurate with the demands of current research and analysis as demonstrated in Chapters Two, Three and Four of this study.

CHAPTER II

Statistical Analysis

> When you can measure what you are speaking about, and express it in numbers, you know something about it; but when you cannot measure it, when you cannot express it in numbers, your knowledge is of a meager and unsatisfactory kind: it may be the beginning of knowledge, but you have scarcely, in your own thoughts, advanced to the state of science.[1]

Introduction

When Barthélemy presented the preliminary publication of the *Dodekapropheton* scroll of the Minor Prophets in 1963[2] his extended analysis of the implications of the καίγε text ranged into 2 Reigns. He demonstrated that this text was not a new translation of the Hebrew as Thackeray had proposed,[3] but was a recension based on an already existing Greek text. Further, he concluded that in the βγ section of Reigns[4] all of the manuscripts, including MS B and congeners MSS y a$_2$, but ex-

---

[1]Lord Kelvin, 1883.

[2]*Devanciers.*

[3]"The Greek Translators of the Four Books of Kings," *JTS* 8 (1907): 262-278. See below for details of the four divisions.

[4]2 Reigns 11:2–3 Reigns 2:11.

cluding the Lucianic manuscripts, share the καίγε text characteristics
established in his study of the Minor Prophets, leaving the Lucianic text
as the sole witness to the Old Greek text.

The problem with this conclusion is that there are no controls, no
way to know whether in 2 Reigns the Lucianic text may not in fact be
witness to some third type of text which is similar to, but also different
from, the Old Greek.

Thus it is necessary first to analyze the relationships in 1 Reigns
where the Old Greek text of MS B is able to provide controls, to ascertain
the affinity between it and the Lucianic manuscripts. If no such
relationship is in evidence there, then the conclusion for 2 Reigns is
thereby placed in jeopardy, especially since the Lucianic manuscripts are
generally regarded as homogeneous throughout 1-4 Reigns.

Beyond that the relation of the Lucianic manuscripts to MS A in
1 Reigns is also studied to see what affinity exists between them and the
hexaplaric text.

Assumptions

Three of the assumptions presented in the Introduction, which are
based on previous scholarship, underlie this analysis. They are that for
1 Reigns: MS B is the best available witness to the Old Greek; MS A is
the prime hexaplaric text; and the whole book was originally the work of
a single translator.

Were it to be demonstrated that either of the collation manu-
scripts (MS B and MS A) did not witness to the claimed text (Old Greek
and hexaplaric respectively) then the comparisons themselves would not
be invalidated *per se* inasmuch as the relationships between the manu-
scripts would still be the same irrespective of their significance, although
the original conclusions drawn from the results would not be valid.

The Bi-sections of the Books of Reigns

In his Schweich lectures of 1920 Thackeray presented the results of his study of the bi-sections of the four books of Reigns[5] which had enabled him, by careful analysis of the text, to isolate distinct strata. On the basis of two syntactical and eight lexicographic features he divided the four books between two separate and distinct translators, one of which he concluded to be an early translation and the other a later one.

By taking into consideration the content of the later translation–stories that spoke adversely concerning David–he concluded that it was supplied to replace text intentionally omitted from the earlier translation for reasons similar to those which motivated the omission of the David and Bathsheba story from the Book of Chronicles. The divisions of the Book, along with the sigla that he used, are as follows:

α = 1 Rgn[6]
$\beta\beta$ = 2 Rgn 1:11–11:1[7]

---

[5]Thackeray usually refers to these books under the rubric of "Kingdoms," though he explains that the meaning of Βασιλεια in Hellenistic times was "Reigns" (*JTS*, vol. 8 [1907], p. 263, note a; *SAJW*, p. 17), which seems to indicate that though he mildly protests the use of the term "Kingdoms" it was already well entrenched. "Reigns" is used (and preferred) in this work, except when quoting from the work of others.

Because most of the Books of the LXX were translated from the Hebrew, it is not surprising to see the Greek Books also referred to from time-to-time by the titles for the Hebrew books. For instance it is traditionally said that Rahlfs, in two of his Studies, analyzed the Lucianic manuscripts of 1-2 Kings, not 3-4 Reigns (or Kingdoms), which occasions no confusion. What is distressing is to find the Greek of 1-2 Samuel referred to as 1-2 Kings, and 1-2 Kings referred to as 3-4 Kings. Such references only create confusion.

[6]Though not cited in the Introduction, this is further evidence of the unity of the translation of 1 Reigns.

[7]The subsequent research of Shenkel (*Chronology*, pp. 117-120) has demonstrated that there is evidence (based on the elimination of the historic presents from the text, one of the characteristics of the καιγε text) to end this section at 9:13 and begin the next at 10:1, though this has not been accepted by all. While Thackeray's conclusions were motivated by theological concerns–the impact of the David and Bathsheba story–Shenkel concentrates on the linguistic features of the text.

βγ = 2 Rgn 11:2–3 Rgn 2:11
γγ = 3 Rgn 2:12–21:43
γδ = 3 Rgn 22 + 4 Rgn

In addition, the siglum βδ is used to refer to the combined passages βγ and γδ which are the two parts of the later stratum.

Theory of Analysis

In this chapter a statistical analysis is made of the interrelationships between MSS B, A and boc₂e₂ to establish their affinities. The degree of affinity that exists between manuscripts is directly proportional to the number of readings shared in common, and is best tested where the readings of the collation manuscript are supported by a minority of the extant witnesses.

Manuscript interrelationships

There are two separate and distinct interrelationships of significance here: that of the manuscripts in the database to one another, and that of the Lucianic manuscripts to MS B and to MS A.

1. Interrelationship of all the manuscripts

This aspect is of fundamental importance because if the interrelationships of the manuscripts listed in B-M are essentially random then attempts at statistical analysis are *a priori* robbed of significance. The question then is: Is there a fundamental interrelationship among the manuscripts, or do they ultimately bear witness to independent translations? Although in this study it is accepted that there is a fundamental interrelationship, because the matter is crucial to the validity of the statistical analysis and has been the center of considerable debate in the past, it is reviewed here in greater depth.

The names that have come to represent the two sides of the issue are Lagarde and Kahle. Although the development of the respective ideas proposed by them has outstripped their original theories, their names have traditionally been retained at the masthead of their respective schools of thought. Central to the debate is the question of whether there ever was a single *Urtext* that underlay the later manuscripts, or whether the process was the reverse, so that out of a number of independent translations one standard text came to the fore.

The name of Lagarde has come to be synonymous with the concept of an original Old Greek version that consisted of the translations of the various books, and was a unified corpus of literature. The point of departure is his three canons for the recreation of the original text of the LXX.[8] There is no discussion *per se* of the question of an *Urtext* in these canons because it was simply assumed, as can be seen from the fact that the discussion begins with the assumption that the texts have become mixed as "the result of an eclectic process." Consequently the discussion turns upon the question of how to get back to the assumed original, a process that Lagarde believed could be achieved by the application of his principles.

This school of thought recognizes that there was a variety of translators with discernibly different styles that contributed to the original work ("His only standard will be his knowledge of the style of the individual translators ..."). From there the Old Greek text in the process of being copied was corrected, edited, redacted, corrupted and added to,

---

[8]*Anmerkungen zur griech. Übersetzung der Proverbien*, p. 3. These canons have been translated by Driver:

"1.   The MSS. of the Greek translation of the OT. are all either immediately or mediately the result of an eclectic process: it follows that he who aims at recovering the original text must follow an eclectic method likewise. His only standard will be his knowledge of the style of the individual translators: his chief aid will be the faculty possessed by him of referring the readings which come before him to their Semitic original, or else of recognizing them as corruptions originating in the Greek.

2.   If a verse or part of a verse appears in both a free and a slavishly literal translation, the former is to be counted the genuine rendering.

3.   If two readings co-exist, of which one expresses the Massoretic text, while the other can only be explained from a text deviating from it, the latter is to be regarded as the original" (*Notes*, p. xliv).

accidentally and intentionally, until there was the wide variety of variants
that we see today in the extant manuscripts. Jellicoe, commenting on the
work of Lagarde says:

> Although fraught with grave difficulties owing to the consistently mixed
> nature of the extant authorities, it would be hard to devise an alternative
> procedure by which–assuming an *Urtext* for the LXX–such a restoration
> could be effected.[9]

This work was carried on by Lagarde's pupil Rahlfs and from
there has blossomed into the Göttingen edition of the LXX which con-
tinues to build on the foundation laid by Lagarde.

On the other hand the name of Kahle is associated with the idea
of multiple independent translations. Kahle's theory was intended to
account for the degree of variation among the Greek texts which he en-
countered, a degree that he believed precluded the possibility of common
origin. Instead he found in his picture of the development of the
Aramaic Targums from multiple independent translations to official texts
an illustration that accorded with his understanding of the development
of the Greek texts. He believed that at the outset there were multiple
translations from Hebrew into Greek to meet local needs, rather than
one (semi-official) translation as pictured in the Letter of Aristeas.[10]
Kahle believed that one of these translations came to be the standard
tradition. His own summary is:

> The task which the Septuagint presents to scholars is not the 'recon-
> struction' of an imaginary 'Urtext' nor the discovery of it, but a careful
> collection and investigation of all the remains and traces of earlier

---

[9]Jellicoe, *SAMS*, p. 8.

[10]Though most of the Letter is clearly apocryphal, it is usually accorded validity in
its description of the origins of the earliest translations from Hebrew into Greek in
Alexandria–at least as far as the Pentateuch is concerned, and possibly more–to meet the
needs of the growing Jewish community there.

versions of the Greek Bible which differed from the Christian standard text.[11]

Outside of Kahle and his pupils this theory has generally not found support, although it did engage the focus of the discipline for some time. Roberts, who recognized "many attractive features" in this theory, nevertheless concluded:

> ... it is not likely that the theory will gain universal acceptance .... [T]here seems to be an absence of strong historical support for it, and there is no reason why that evidence should have been suppressed had it ever existed."[12]

In reference to the Targum analogy in particular Katz says:

> ... I undertook to demonstrate that the comparison with the Targums rested on loose analogies, that the several books of the LXX at their first stage disclose the individual traits of their authors, that the wealth of variants is perplexing only as long as they are neither grouped nor analyzed, and that most of them, including the indirect quotations, derive from well-known secondary recensions and are neither LXX nor early.[13]

Tov has focused on the similarities between these two approaches and suggested a third synthetic view which he characterizes as a theory of "multiple textual traditions." He says:

> ... one Greek translation must be presupposed as the base of the manuscripts of most, if not all, the books of the LXX. The original wording of this translation was not long preserved in a pure form. With the beginning of the textual transmission of the original translation in different scrolls it split into several secondary textual traditions, since

---

[11]*Cairo Geniza*, p. 264. One of the frustrations experienced by scholars has been the failure of Kahle to identify what he understood to be encompassed by what he termed "the Christian standard text."

[12]*OTTV*, p. 113. Similar to this is the comment of Katz: "Struck by the obvious irrelevance of this new branch of study as presented in *The Cairo Geniza*, I subjected it to a searching study, only to find out that it involved no cogent argument, but merely a mass of uncoordinated information" (*SITS*, p. 50).

[13]Ibid.

various types of corrections (mainly towards the Hebrew) were inserted in the individual scrolls. Presumably these textual traditions continued to develop.[14]

While it is true that the issue was a live one for some time, there is now a consensus in favor of the Lagardian principles, especially in the light of the discovery and publication of the Qumran material and the Greek *Dodekapropheton* scroll from Nahal Hever. Kahle appealed to both of these as evidencing support for his theory,[15] but scholarship has generally not been convinced. Cross's assessment in the light of the Qumran material is that "Attacks on Lagarde's position show at most that he overstates his case."[16] Barthélemy, in his publication of the *Dodeka-propheton* scroll, discussed the implications for Kahle's theory that arose from the nature of the contents of the scroll, and he concluded that the manuscript does not support the theory.[17]

---

[14]*Text-critical Use*, pp. 41-42. Tov goes on to say "On the basis of this theory, four stages in the development of the text of the LXX can be recognized:
1.   The original translation.
2.   A multitude of textual traditions resulting from the insertion of corrections (mainly towards the Hebrew) in all known individual scrolls in the pre-Christian period, and to a lesser extent in the first century C.E.
3.   Textual stabilization in the first and second centuries C.E., due to the perpetuation of some textual traditions and the discontinuation of others.
4.   The creation of new textual groups and the corruption of existing ones through the influence of the revisions of Origen and Lucian in the third and fourth centuries C.E." (ibid., p. 42).

Point one above recognizes that one original translation underlies all the rest, and points two through four account for the variety of variants that Kahle noted, as well as the later standardization (or 'stabilization' as Tov calls it) of the text.

[15]*Cairo Geniza*, pp. 209-239.

[16]*ALQ²*, p. 170, n. 13.

[17]Because of its importance the full text of his final paragraph is included. "Sur un plan plus général nous pouvons conclure avec fermeté que cette découverte n'apporte aucun fondement à la thèse des targums grecs chère à KAHLE. Cette hypothèse demeurera une vue de l'esprit tant que des analyses méticuleuses ne l'auront pas fondée sur des cas précis. Encore convient-il de ne pas oublier que la tradition textuelle de

In his dissertation Brock focuses on that aspect of Kahle's theory that suggests that the existence of variants is evidence of multiple translations, especially as Brock was able to put it to the test in connection with 1 Reigns. He points out first that little if any coherent evidence has ever been adduced for the theory, and second–and more important–the total impracticability of such a theory. He concludes:

> As far as I Kms is concerned, the matter in common between *L*[ucian] and LXX rell is so great that it would have required a Philonic miracle (and then not a very competent one, in view of the actual divergences) to have brought about such a close identity of two different translations. Consequently it may be safely assumed that our Greek text of I Kms goes back to a single translation: if there did ever exist another one, or other ones, the only traces they can be supposed to have left will be in individual passages or variants where they have contaminated the surviving translation (or manuscripts of this).[18]

The scholarship has been examined at some length, even though Brock's conclusion is now more than twenty years old, because it is crucial to this study. If there were to be no underlying fundamental relationship between the Greek manuscripts beyond the fact that they were all translated from the same (or a similar) Hebrew text, then any

---

chaque livre de la Bible grecque pose des problèmes particuliers, ce qui interdira d'emblée toute généralisation. Pour ce qui est du Dodécaprophéton, l'auteur de notre recension travaillait déjà au début de notre ère sur un texte dont les leçons particulières se retrouveraient presque toutes dans l'apparat critique de ZIEGLER" (*Devanciers*, p. 272).

Ulrich accepts Barthélemy's conclusions, commenting: "On the basis of the Minor Prophets scroll, Barthélemy seems to have effectively laid to rest Kahle's 'Targumic' theory as the principal explanation of LXX origins ...." (*Qumran*, p. 29).

After assessing the evidence, Shenkel is uncompromising: "The classic approach of the Lagardian school to Septuagint research is adopted in the present study as a working hypothesis. There was one original translation of a Hebrew text of Samuel and Kings into Greek" (*Chronology*, p. 5).

[18]"Recensions," p. 31. It should be noted that Brock recognizes that those portions of chapters 17-18 (and presumably the single verse of 23:12 which belongs in the same tradition, although he does not specifically address the matter) not found in MS B and congeners are the work of a later hand, but that this fact does not weaken the argument for the unity of the rest of the translation because they are clearly a separate consideration.

statistical analysis based upon establishing the number of readings shared in common would be largely meaningless, even if there were to be a degree–even a high degree–of agreement among the manuscripts.

Thus it is not enough to adopt a pragmatic approach based on the degree of agreement; rather it is necessary to note that for 1 Reigns (and more besides) there is no evidence for, or substance to, the theory that the extant witnesses are at their core independent of one another; that the evidence–and lack of any substantive contrary evidence–points to an original set of translations that are commonly referred to as "Septuagint" and "Old Greek."[19]

2. Interrelationship of MSS boc_2e_2, B and A

Accepting the validity of the Lagardian principles it follows that behind each of the manuscripts in the corpus, apart from those representing known later translations, there is one original Old Greek text. However, the relationship of any single manuscript (or group(s) of manuscripts) to any other, and the degree to which the Old Greek can be recovered, will vary considerably all the way from those manuscripts that are the Old Greek in an essentially pure form by all the criteria available today, to those whose text is not easily recognizable because of the addition of such as hexaplaric materials and/or scribal emendations of whatever kind, whether intentional or unintentional, that have accrued in the copying/editing process.[20]

---

[19]Shenkel comments: "The term 'Old Greek' is used for the original translation into Greek ... in preference to the term 'Septuagint' which is often used loosely to designate the entire Greek version" (*Shenkel*, Chronology, p. 124, n. 2). Kraft suggests that "... it is more accurate to speak of the oldest recoverable Greek form of each section/book ..." ("Septuagint: Earliest Greek Versions," *IDBS*, p. 811).

[20]Skeat observes that "Because a manuscript is full of errors due to dictation, it does not follow that it gives us a bad text; on the contrary, in most of the manuscripts which we have been considering in detail, the misspellings and other blunders are purely superficial, and when they are stripped off, the resultant texts are very good indeed" ("Use of Dictation," p. 206).

When two manuscripts or groups of manuscripts which have this underlying fundamental relationship are compared there are two ways to describe the relationship: by comparison or by contrast. Thus it is with the manuscripts under consideration here. On the one hand MSS boc_2e_2 have been compared with MS B as the Old Greek referent. Writers such as Rahlfs, Barthélemy, Tov, Cross and Wevers[21] have emphasized the points of similarity; while Kraft[22] on the other hand has contrasted the

---

Two examples of manuscripts in 1 Reigns that have suffered in this fashion are MS g and MS v which abound with frequent (and sometimes amusing) orthographic variants, but given the reference points available from the other manuscripts these factors are controllable.

[21]In his justly renowned *Septuaginta-Studien* vols. 1 and 3, Rahlfs studied the Lucianic text in 1-2 Kings [= 3-4 Reigns]. Moore provides the following summary as it pertains to the current discussion: "... Rahlfs finds that, of the witnesses in our hands, the text underlying the recension of Lucian stands closest to B, and to the Ethiopic version in the older and purer form represented by Dillmann's Codd. S and A, the affinity of which to B in Kings has long been known. This text was 'pre-hexaplar,' and Lucian is sometimes, especially in 1 Kings, an important witness to this text, by the side of B, Aeth" ("Recensions," p. 61; see also: Driver, *Notes*, p. xlviii-l; Metzger, *Chapters*, p. 11; Ulrich, *Qumran*, p. 33).
Barthélemy: "C'est essentiellement la Septante ancienne, plus ou moins abâtardie et corrompue" (*Devanciers*, p. 127).
Tov: "Barthélemy and Tov regard this substratum as the Old Greek translation of Samuel-Kings, now lost, which often agreed with 4Q Sam[ab]" ("Septuagint," *IDBS*, p. 809).
Cross: "The proto-Lucianic text in Samuel in my view was essentially G with intruded Palestinian readings ...." ("Local Texts," p. 315).
Wevers: "There is to my mind no doubt that the Antiochian text was an early revision of the Septuagint text. That it was a revision rather than a separate translation can be demonstrated from a careful study of the Lucianic text. No two separate translations could have made the same peculiar mistranslations in so many places ..." ("Proto-Septuagint," p. 69).

[22]Commenting on Barthélemy's hypothesis that in βγ the Lucianic manuscripts alone contain the Old Greek, Kraft says: "... the identification of MSS boc_2e_2 with the 'ancient Alexandrian Version' is highly questionable in view of the fact that even in the non-καιγε sections which are preserved by most Greek manuscripts (e.g. 1 Sam), there is a characteristic *difference* between the majority text ('LXX') and MSS boc_2e_2–and B[arthélemy] himself accepts the majority text as basically 'LXX' in these sections" (*Gnomon* 37, p. 482; emphasis his).

two texts. It is important to note that while these two perspectives do reflect a difference of opinion, it is possible for both aspects to be correct–or better, that they differ with respect to emphases determined by the context of the comments rather than from any failure to understand the texts.[23]

For 1 Reigns there are 20,160 words in the Rahlfs text which is a good approximation to the Old Greek text. In the case of MS B the number of B readings supported by no more than 15 other manuscripts[24] is 926,[25] or just under 5% of the total. Thus one can speak of textual affinity in one context, and in another context to speak of textual divergence.

Three relationships are under study here–that between MS B and the Lucianic text, that between MS B and MS A, and that between MS A and the Lucianic text. The first has attracted the most attention because of the belief that Lucianic studies in Reigns hold an important key, via the analysis of the underlying Old Greek text, to the unlocking of the Hebrew Vorlage.[26] The second is next in importance, again primarily

---

[23]That this is so is seen in the comment of Shenkel who recognizes both similarities and differences: "Proto-Lucian differs from the Old Greek in a number of readings, but in general has the same order and structuring" (*Chronology*, p. 6).

Fernández Marcos takes as basic that "the Antiochian text is first and foremost Septuagint, that is, it shares with the Old Greek all its remarkable differences as against the Masoretic text .... We cannot lose sight of this in everything we say about its peculiarities" ("Literary and Editorial Features," p. 289).

[24]This figure is selected because it represents just over half of the manuscripts in the database used for statistical analysis (as noted above, some manuscripts were included on the authority of H-P which are not used for the statistical analysis).

[25]In the database MS B (and congeners) is listed as "omitting" the hexaplaric material. This total does not include these "omissions."

[26]Abercrombie is correct when he says "The text critic aims at recovering the oldest or most authentic wording of a document from the extant material–the original if possible" (*Literary Analysis*, p. 85). Though this present study of the Lucianic manuscripts stops short of recreating the Hebrew *Vorlage* it does essentially recreate the Greek archetype of the five Lucianic manuscripts.

in connection with the underlying Old Greek, although in the comparison of MS B and MS A attention has also been focused on the absence of the hexaplaric material from MS B. The third relationship has attracted little comment at the Old Greek level, although there has been interest in the Lucianic manuscripts as witnesses to the hexaplaric material, especially as evidenced by MS c_2 which is the prime text outside of MSS Acx for hexaplaric signs in 1 Reigns.[27]

In this connection Brock, Shenkel, and Thackeray have commented on the relationship between MSS A and B, seeing a close relationship between them.[28]

The synthesis of these comments leads naturally to the conclusion that there is a fundamentally close relationship between all of these manuscripts–boc₂e₂, B and A–at the Old Greek level, even to the extent of sharing a common stock. It remains for the statistical analysis to reveal whether or not this is so, and if so, to what extent.

Method

By means of computer programs, the minority readings of the two collation manuscripts–readings supported by less than half the manuscripts in the database–were extracted. B-M selected thirty-two manuscripts for inclusion in their edition of 1 Reigns, so that fifteen represents

---

[27]Note that this does not mean that MS c_2 is the prime hexaplaric witness outside of MSS Acx, only that it is the prime witness to the signs.

[28]Brock: "In non-hexaplaric readings O [=Acx] Arm are very close to Bya_2 Eth" ("Recensions," p. 15).

Shenkel: "The best manuscript of the Books of Samuel and Kings for both the Old Greek and the K[aige] R[ecension] is the Codex Vaticanus. The text displayed by this manuscript is commonly conceded to be pre-hexaplaric, which means that it, or a closely related text form, served as the basic text for Origen's recensional activity" (*Chronology*, p. 19).

Thackeray: "The A text ... is a recension of the shorter B text, to bring it into line with the revised Hebrew; the additional matter, absent from B, being supplied mainly from Aquila, whose peculiarities are unmistakable" (*SAJW*, p. 16).

one less than half. However, with 'b' in the main representing essentially the same text in two manuscripts, the total is counted at thirty-one, and a minority at fourteen (again, one less than half).

A number of decisions needed to be made in advance at the computer programming level, relative to the inclusion or exclusion of data, so that the results would be accurate. They are detailed below:

a. The readings of the first hand are consistently preferred over later hands. Walters has written at length on this matter, pointing out that in the case of MS B the later hands extend through the eleventh century. It was of concern to him that B-M took no cognizance of this matter and presented the readings of the later hands as if they were all of a kind with the first hand.[29] As far as the Lucianic manuscripts are concerned it is not known when the later hands date from, although the manuscripts date from the tenth to fourteenth centuries. Because of the uncertainty of the origin and significance of later readings as a whole, it was decided to prefer the readings of the original hand over later hands as a precautionary step. This includes readings marked by the asterisk over against those marked as [a] or [b], as well 'in-text' readings over against marginal glosses.

b. The base text for the database is Rahlfs' reconstruction of the Old Greek. While this text is largely based on MS B, it does not follow MS B exactly. As a result the database layout tags base text words lacking in MS B, for whatever reason, as omissions by MS B, irrespective of whether these words were ever a part of MS B. Consequently, because such omissions are not in fact B readings, they are not included in the statistics.

---

[29]Walters, *TOTS*, pp. 7,8; 275-277.

c. Following MS B, the Rahlfs' text, does not contain the hexaplaric material found in chapters 17-18[30] and 23:12. For these passages a base text for collation purposes was supplied from MS A.[31] In the analysis the statistics derived from this data are listed and studied separately from the main body of the statistical material to prevent contamination.[32]

There are methodological objections to filling the lacunae in one manuscript with the text of another, if the first is chosen solely because it is an uncial, not for its textual profile.[33] Clearly there is a fundamental difference between the two manuscripts–B and A–as evidenced by this addition/omission situation.

In the light of this it is appropriate to continue in the same spirit and treat the hexaplaric passages separately. As it turned out from the actual analysis, though the majority of the manuscripts have text for these passages, especially chapter seventeen, they exhibit an unusually high degree of independence from MS A (as the prime hexaplaric exemplar and as base text).

d. Where readings of the collation manuscript agree with the base text, but are in a different order, they are tagged as a transposition in the database. In this case all manuscripts that support the transposed read-

---

[30]See p. 13, n. 32.

[31]In addition, the Rahlfs reconstruction of the OG does not include 13:1 which falls within a physical lacuna of MS A (a leaf of the codex is missing). In this case the base text is taken from MSS cx, the closest congeners to MS A, a reading also shared by MSS boc₂e₂ qz fm g. Although it is probable that MS A shared this reading, the statistics have been confined to the extant A readings, and so this verse is also not included in the statistical analysis.

[32]This affects only MS A as base text in these passages, and MS B as "omitting" the readings.

[33]In defence of both Rahlfs and B-M it needs to be pointed out that neither the Rahlfs text nor the Cambridge text contains these passages. In the database they were added from the apparatus of B-M where the text of MS A is printed at the head of each verse, or in its absence, the text of its closest congeners.

ing of MS B are counted, irrespective of whether their reading is actually a transposition. The situation arises when some manuscripts transpose while others have the reading twice, once in the base text order, and once in transposition.

e. Omission statistics are not included in the analysis since it is not possible to distinguish between all the various types of omissions such as physical lacunae and haplography on the one hand, and the fact that the reading of the collation manuscript never was part of the tradition of the "omitting" manuscript.[34]

f. An upper limit is set for the inclusion of readings in the analysis: only readings of the two collation manuscripts supported by less than a majority of the database manuscripts are included. At the lower limit the readings of the collation manuscript that have no external support (unique readings) are excluded because this is a comparative analysis, and such readings have no comparison.[35]

---

[34]For details of the limitations of the omissions category see p. 23-25.

[35]The following lists the number of unique readings for each collation manuscript by database categories:

B	base text	18
	omissions	29
	substitutions	43
	transpositions	2
	additions	9
A	base text	1
	base text (hex)	12
	omissions	131
	substitutions	313
	transpositions	31
	additions	94

g. To provide greater depth of analysis, in addition to the two summary tables, one each for MS B and MS A,[36] there are tables for the hexaplaric material—one for the additions alone from MS A, and one for the totals without the additions.

Theoretical Limits

It needs to be understood from the outset that the statistics are only significant in relation to the collation manuscript. While it is reasonable to expect that the statistics for individual members of a family will be close to each other inasmuch as they have been perceived consistently to share readings independent of these statistical analyses, no precise evaluation of the family groupings is possible on the basis of comparison with a manuscript external to that family. This relationship can only be assessed statistically when the family, or a member of the family, is the basis of the collation.

Further, it is not possible to reach qualitative conclusions solely on the basis of statistical analysis. Thus many questions that are legitimate in themselves are not appropriate in this context, such as: 'Which is the better/correct reading?' Nor is the problem a lack of statistical data, or of sophistication in the analysis. A gulf is as it were fixed between these two different types of questions.

Format of the Tables

The statistics are presented in a series of tables, all of which have the same format. In the left column, arranged vertically, are the three families included in the analysis. The collation manuscript is first, followed by the other two members of its family. Next are the members of the Lucianic family in alphabetical order, with the two b manuscripts

---

[36]These two tables include the statistics from the following database categories: base text, substitutions, transpositions, and additions.

listed individually. Finally the other collation manuscript and its family are listed.

The next column contains first the number of minority readings of the collation manuscript[37] that are attested by 13 or less other manuscripts[38] (for a total of 14 manuscripts[39]), and then the number of times the selected manuscripts share these readings.

The final column presents the total for each manuscript as a percentage of the collation manuscript total.

Analysis of the Statistics

1. Ms B as the collation manuscript

Table 2

Mss	Total Minority Readings	Total as % of B
B	673	100.00
y	418	62.11
a_2	457	67.90
b'	66	9.81
b	71	10.55
o	81	12.04
c_2	79	11.74
e_2	69	10.25
A	256	38.04
c	202	30.01
x	218	32.39

---

[37]As noted above, this total does not include the unique readings of the collation manuscript.

[38]While the statistics listed in the tables are limited to the three families, the original analysis included all of the 31 manuscripts in the database. Not included were the H-P manuscripts which are only occasionally cited by B-M.

[39]As noted, this figure represents a minority of the database manuscripts.

As is to be expected, the greatest affinity among the manuscripts under study is that between MS B and its congeners, MSS ya$_2$, at approximately 65%, since it is such affinity that marked them as members of the group in the first place.

The next closest is MS A, at just under 40%, with MSS c x the next highest, so that both the individual manuscript (A) and the family (c x) are the closest to MS B, and its family (y a$_2$) of the manuscripts under study.[40]

One of the well-known characteristics of MS A is its frequent orthographic variants that set it apart from all of the manuscripts, including its congeners, indicating that these readings arose subsequent to the branching of MSS c x. Were these anomalies, that reflect copyist error, not differences of textual traditions, able to be eliminated, the affinity with MS B would be even closer.

What was not expected is to find that the Lucianic manuscripts barely reach into the mid-teens, and are the lowest group to the extent that no clear relationship is in evidence between them and MS B in these readings. In fact, not only are the Lucianic manuscripts lower than MSS A c x, they are the lowest of all of the families in the database. The only other manuscripts with comparable low percentages are those with major physical lacunae.

---

[40]This is true not only of the manuscripts included in this limited study, but is true of all the manuscripts in the database. The next closest is MS n at just under 30%.

2. MS *A as the collation manuscript*

Table 3

Mss	Total Minority Readings	Total as % of A
A	1173	100.00
c	698	59.51
x	719	61.30
b′	332	28.30
b	334	28.47
o	323	27.54
c_2	358	30.52
e_2	317	27.02
B	255	21.74
y	245	20.89
a_2	257	21.91

The situation here is more complex than it was for MS B. There the collation was to a text believed to represent the Old Greek and hence was a short text with additions a relatively minor category. Here the text is known to be hexaplaric, a rubric that means primarily that it is a longer text, having been harmonized by Origen to the Hebrew text. Hence to compare the Lucianic manuscripts to MS A in a meaningful way that will correspond to the comparison made to MS B requires a further division in the 'totals' figures between those of additions and the rest of the statistics that are included. That way the remaining figures pertain primarily to the base text here as they did in the case of MS B.

3. MS A as the collation manuscript: Additions

Table 4

Mss	Total Minority Readings	Total as % of A
A	467	100.00
c	322	68.95
x	328	70.24
b′	207	44.33
b	211	45.18
o	202	43.25
c_2	237	50.75
e_2	197	42.18
B	5	1.07
y	17	3.64
a_2	13	2.78

This table was created by omitting the statistics from the additions database category. Rahlfs' goal in creating his LXX text was to represent the Old Greek as faithfully as possible. To the extent that he was successful–and it is a good representation–the additions in MS A, the prime exemplar of Origen's text, record the hexaplaric (and other) additions to the Old Greek text.[41]

Were there to have been any question as to whether the Lucianic manuscripts have been 'contaminated' by hexaplaric readings this table dispels that doubt. Approximately 45% of the A minority readings that

---

[41]It is not known precisely how many of these additions are in fact hexaplaric. What is known is that the principle effect of Origen's work was to increase the length of the text as he added readings to correspond with those Hebrew readings currently not represented in his Greek text. Therefore this category is the repository of these additions, whatever other additions may also be here.

Thus, by treating the additions separately, we have a good approximation of the degree of hexaplaric contamination in the Lucianic manuscripts *vis-à-vis* MS A, and, as anticipated, the absence of that contamination in MS B.

are not unique to A are shared by the Lucianic manuscripts, the highest
affinity of the categories.

Thus, where MS A witnesses to a text longer than MS B (except for
5 readings they share), almost half of those readings are shared by the
Lucianic group.

4. MS A as the collation manuscript: Totals Without Additions

Table 5

Mss	Total Minority Readings	Total as % of A
A	706	100.00
c	376	53.26
x	391	55.38
b′	125	17.71
b	123	17.42
o	121	17.14
c_2	121	17.14
e_2	120	17.00
B	250	35.41
y	228	32.29
a_2	244	34.56

At first glance, it may seem as though once the additions have
been removed, the remaining statistics would represent the Old Greek.
In fact the transmission of the text was much more complex than that,
impacting at every level.

It is clear from the table that, apart from the (hexaplaric)
additions, the B group has significantly stronger affinity with MS A than
does the Lucianic group. In addition, note that the percentages for the
A group compared to MS B are essentially the same as the B group com-
pared to MS A, and are in the range of 35%.

From this it can be seen that, apart from the hexaplaric additions, the B group has significantly stronger affinity with MS A than does the Lucianic group, while the previous table shows that the Lucianic manuscripts have a strong affinity with the hexaplaric additions of MS A.

Conclusions

The primary objective of this study was to analyze the relationship between the Lucianic manuscripts and the Old Greek of 1 Reigns as represented by the minority readings of MS B. On the basis of the statistics it can be categorically stated that there is no relationship in evidence between them. Of all the families or individual manuscripts included in the database no manuscripts show less affinity than the Lucianic manuscripts except for individual manuscripts that have major physical lacunae.

Tov suggested that rather than being *the* Old Greek, the Lucianic manuscripts may be *an* Old Greek text. While this may have been intended as no more than a facetious remark, it is now possible to put even such suggestions aside. The Lucianic text is not Old Greek by the criteria that have led to the conclusion that MS B is Old Greek.

On the other hand Cross suggested that the Lucianic text is at most "a light revision of the Old Greek, consisting of occasional corrections to the closely allied Palestinian text."[42] In the light of the research this does not go far enough.

It may then be asked whether the Lucianic text may not after all be the representative of the Old Greek, and the text of MS B and congeners be the recension. It was to address this issue that MS A and congeners were included in the study.

Shenkel commented of MS B "that it, or a closely related text form, served as the basic text for Origen's recensional activity."[43] If Shenkel

---

[42]"Local Texts," p. 319, n. 30. These comments apply to both Books of Samuel, not just the βγ section (p. 312).

[43]*Chronology*, p. 19.

is correct, then it is obvious that the Lucianic text cannot be the basis, because it is not "a closely related text form." However, that fact in itself does not address the whole issue, because it is not sufficient to note the absence of affinity between MS B and the Lucianic manuscripts, or between them and MS A, affinity must also be established between MS B and MS A for the claim to be true.

The congeners of MS B share approximately 60-70% of its readings. The next closest manuscript is MS A at 38%. Outside of MSS y a₂, MS A is the closest overall to MS B of all of the manuscripts in the database.[44] Further corroborative evidence is supplied from the analysis based on MS A. Outside of the hexaplaric additions,[45] the congeners of MS A share approximately 55% of the A readings, while MS B shares 35% of them, results comparable to, and compatible with, those for MS B. In contrast, the Lucianic manuscripts are within a percentage point of each other at a mere 17%.

Thus the statistics support Shenkel's claim that the hexaplaric readings were added to a text similar to MS B. In the light of this, there is no reason to disturb that relationship in an effort to retain the Lucianic manuscripts as Old Greek.

Further, with the Lucianic texts not bearing any special relationship to the Old Greek in 1 Reigns, it is no longer possible to see them as the sole witnesses to the Old Greek in the καίγε passages, especially since Barthélemy drew on parallels from 1 Reigns to show that these manuscripts share the same translation characteristics in both the καίγε and the non-καίγε passages.

This means that in the καίγε passages there are two witnesses to the text, the majority recension contained in all the manuscripts except

---

[44]For further details, see the full statistics in the Appendix.

[45]These additions do not include the large block of text in chapters 17, 18 (the David and Goliath pericope) that was not part of the original Old Greek Text. Rather, they are the hexaplaric additions that occur throughout the rest of the book of 1 Reigns.

the Lucianic, and the Lucianic recension which is non-καίγε but also not Old Greek.

In the light of these facts it can be seen that the creation of the Göttingen edition for the καίγε passages will be difficult inasmuch as no witness to the Old Greek has survived.

What then of the Old Greek readings that have traditionally been claimed for MSS b o c₂ e₂? In general, of course, any manuscript is capable of containing earlier readings, either by their having been retained in the textual tradition, or by harmonization. However, in the light ot these statistics, one cannot continue with the wholesale assumption that where there are divergent readings, the Lucianic reading probably retains the Old Greek reading. The burden of proof, while not excluding that possibility, now lies against such an assumption.

What then of Tov's suggestion that the Lucianic text is *an* Old Greek rather than *the* Old Greek text? Could it have something to offer after all? Scholars have come to look upon the Lucianic text as a rich source of early readings. Is it possible to retain this position?

The answer hinges upon what is meant by the term Old Greek. If the term is inclusive of manuscripts as divergent as MS B and the Lucianic manuscripts, then it takes on a meaning quite different from the customary usage. Yet this is what would be necessary to retain the Lucianic manuscripts as Old Greek.

Ironically, this takes us back into the murky waters of Kahle's claim that originally there were a number of independent translations, and only in time did one standard translation emerge. However, the statistics do not substantiate this idea.

Inclusion in the analysis was limited to minority readings of the collation manuscripts. As the total for inclusion is progressively raised more manuscripts are included, more readings are shared in common. There is a common stock of readings, evidence of common origin, and these form the bulk of the readings.

It is easy to overlook just how much these manuscripts do in fact share in common. To this end it is helpful to spend time studying later translations such as those of Aquila and Symmachus that were part of Origen's Hexapla. Not only is the vocabulary different, the syntax is different, the word order is different.

The Lucianic manuscripts do not represent an independent translation. They are not *an* Old Greek text in the sense of an independent translation. They stand firmly in *the* Old Greek tradition, albeit as a witness to recensional activity.

CHAPTER III

Analysis of the Lucianic Majority Variants

Nous nous trouvons ainsi placés devant tant de facteurs distincts qu'une mise en équation des données fournies par l'apparat critique de Brooke-McLean semble une entreprise presque désespérée.[1]

In this chapter the Lucianic majority variants are analyzed. Virtually every detail and nuance of the manuscripts for the thirty-one chapters of 1 Reigns is available for the study, but to attempt to analyze everything would result in focusing on nothing. Consequently the analysis is limited in accord with the bounds of this study and yet is comprehensive enough to provide a synopsis of the distinctive features.

Theoretical Considerations

1. Selection of Data for Analysis

It is accepted as a principle that readings that are unique or are supported by a minority of the manuscripts in the database are more characteristic of a manuscript or family of manuscripts than readings that have wider (majority) support. As was seen in Chapter Two in the case of MS B less than 5% of the B readings are minority readings.[2] The rest are shared by a majority of the manuscripts included in the database.

---

[1]"Because we are thus confronted by so many distinct factors, an evaluation of the data furnished by Brooke-McLean's critical apparatus would seem to be an [almost] futile undertaking" (Barthélemy, "Reexamination," pp. 30-31).

[2]See p. 40.

For this database the cut-off point for minority readings in any manuscript or family of manuscripts is fourteen manuscripts, one less than half the 31 manuscripts. However it was found desirable to limit the data included in this analysis further within this broad category because of the large number of readings which this initial breakdown admits. Accordingly the level of inclusion for the Lucianic manuscripts was lowered from fourteen to only include the Lucianic manuscript(s) and a maximum of six non-Lucianic manuscripts[3] (or a maximum of one third of the total manuscripts).[4]

2. Division of the Data

Having accepted these variants it remained to divide them into meaningful categories that were in turn more manageable, in preparation for the analysis. The first division was between the (Lucianic) readings supported by a majority of the Lucianic manuscripts (three or more), and those supported by a minority of them (two or one).[5] This division forms the basis for the analyses in Chapters III and IV.

---

[3]If only one Lucianic manuscript has a reading, then the maximum is seven manuscripts, if there are four, then it is ten. This way the level of support is held constant, and does not vary upwards as fewer Lucianic manuscripts are included. ·

[4]The same exclusions are made for the data in this analysis as were made in Chapter Two. See pp. 42-45 for details.

[5]The readings which B-M labelled as "b are supported by both MS b′ and MS b. When both of these manuscripts share a reading—as in b′oc$_2$, be$_2$—they only count once for classifying as majority or minority, but count twice when they have separate readings. In practice this is only a factor in minority readings inasmuch as there can only be one majority reading per variant unit, but there can be several minority readings including separate b readings, such as b′o, be$_2$.

Even when this was done there was still need for further classification, so each of the two divisions–majority Lucianic variants, and minority Lucianic variants–was divided between the five database categories.[6]

Within each of these ten categories–five database categories for both majority and minority variants–there is one further division: that between single word variants, and multiple word variants. This is done to maintain the integrity of the longer variants which would otherwise lose their significance divided into single words.

3. Method of analysis

Even when the selected data is divided in this way, a considerable body of variants still remains. To help visualize the information three statistical analyses are made of the variants in each category.

The first table is limited to the Lucianic manuscripts and lists the support for each applicable combination (such as boc_2e_2, boc_2, bc_2e_2, oc_2e_2 for the majority variants; and bo, c_2e_2, bc_2 b for the minority variants) of the Lucianic manuscripts.[7]

Not every partial combination (such as bc_2e_2, oc_2e_2) in one table will have a corresponding entry (o, b) in the other. First, some variants have corresponding readings that are (non-Lucianic) majority readings and so are not included.[8] The second point is a refinement of the first: Lucianic readings that are supported by 14 or less manuscripts, but more than six manuscripts, are also excluded because of the (arbitrarily) low

---

[6]See pp. 22-27 for details. Because the base text (of the database) is neither MS B in its entirety, nor "the Old Greek," but is instead Rahlfs' text, some guidance is given throughout this study of the particular characteristics of each category. This serves as a guide in understanding how to work with the CATSS database in it present form.

[7]Mss b′ and *b* are not distinguished in this table in order to keep the permutations within manageable and meaningful proportions.

[8]At 13:17 MSS $oc_2\text{*}e_2$ z have πηγην, while MSS $bc_2\text{*}$ read γην with the (non-Lucianic) majority. Thus the first reading is included in the analysis because of its low support, but the second is not included, even though it is the reading of MSS $bc_2\text{*}$, because it is supported by a majority of all the database manuscripts.

cut-off point adopted above.[9] This is helpful to keep in mind in under-
standing the tables correctly.

In the second table all of the manuscripts in the database are
listed, grouped vertically by family, with the tabulation of their support
for the Lucianic readings in that (database) category. There are no per-
centages with these statistics as there were in Chapter Two,[10] because
there is no one figure for the Lucianic manuscripts as the point of com-
parison upon which to base percentages. Inasmuch as there is only one
majority reading per variant unit, b′ and b are not distinguished in this
table for majority statistics, but they are listed separately for the minority
readings.

The final table is an analysis of the frequency of the various parts
of speech in that category. These are included because they provide an
overall perspective on types of editorial changes.

The analysis of each set of Lucianic variants is completed by a
synoptic survey. In this survey types of variants are described in broad
categories with examples where appropriate. Above all there is a sensi-
tivity to characteristics and significant trends that are present in the text.
In this way some signposts are located through the text as guides to the
study of the critical text in Volume One.

The Lucianic majority readings, selected according to the guide-
lines discussed above, are studied first because they establish the nature
of the recension.

----

[9]Because of these restrictions some aspects of the Lucianic manuscripts are left
unresearched. One such area is the body of Lucianic readings which are shared in
common with the majority of the manuscripts in the database. Another is the analysis of
each individual Lucianic manuscript in its own right, independent of the others.

[10]See pp. 46-50.

Analysis of the Majority Variants
  1. Base text readings[11]
    a. statistical analysis

This is the smallest group among the majority variants due to the lack of agreement between the Lucianic manuscripts and MS B, as studied in Chapter Two.

Table 6

Lucianic Base Text Majority Readings

boc_2e_2	34	$b\ c_2e_2$	2
boc_2	5	oc_2e_2	3
$bo\ e_2$	2		

Total: 46

Table 7

Non-Lucianic Support for Lucianic Majority Base Text Readings

b	43	B	38	d	3	e	4	M	1
o	44	y	21	l	0	f	1	N	4
c_2	44	a_2	20	p	2	m	0	a	7
e_2	41			q	1	s	2	g	2
				t	2	w	3	h	5
				z	5			i	10
		A	12					j	1
		c	14					n	4
		x	16					v	2
								b_2	3

The only family that stands out in this table is the B group, but it is only close because Rahlfs used it as the basis for his text, with any relation to the Lucianic manuscripts usually being coincidental. Thus it

---

[11]The data for this category has been limited to the Old Greek material. Where the Rahlfs text, on the basis of the Old Greek, does not have verses which the Hebrew text has, the text from the B-M apparatus (usually MS A) was used in the database as the base text so that the hexaplaric variants could be grouped around it. Although some of these readings would qualify on this basis for inclusion here, none have been considered.

is not to be expected that MS B will have any such affinity beyond this category. The only other group to show affinity is the A group, but again it is because Rahlfs granted it second place after MS B, as seen in Chapter Two.

Beyond these two groups the only other manuscript that shows any relationship is MS i. Whether this is significant or not will only be apparent as further categories are studied, inasmuch as what affinity there is could well be with manuscripts A or B.

b. synoptic survey

Table 8

Base Text Range of Variants

Adjectives	0	Names	11	Preposit's	4
Adverbs	0	Nouns	4	Pronouns	4
Articles	6	Numbers	0	Translit's	0
Conjunct's	6	Particles	2	Verbs	9
Interject's	0				

The largest group in the above table is proper names. In the past one of the major methods used to establish manuscript families in 1 Reigns was to study manuscript readings grouped around proper names.[12]

1. single word readings

The first study is of the eleven proper names,[13] which are presented with the full list of the variant forms for each name.

1:9 Σηλω boc₂e₂ Ba₂ Mg] Σηλωμ y A dpqtz efmsw Nahivb₂ : Σιλω v : > cx [*but they have* Σηλωμ, *a virt. tran.*] |

---

[12]See S.J. McGarry, "Early Revisions of the Septuagint Text," (*Proceedings of the Catholic Biblical Association of America*, 1938), pp. 29-35.

[13]Brock, in the Appendix to his dissertation, catalogs and considers all the proper names in 1 Reigns ("Recensions," pp. 316-352).

7:11 Βαιθχορ boc₂e₂ B sw Ngh*] Βεθχορ a₂ : Βαιθχωρ pqtz e nb₂ : Βεθχωρ f : Βηθχωρ On-gr : Βαιθχθορ hᵇ : Βεθχορι i : Βαιχθωρ d : Βεχθωρ cx : Βαιχωρ a : Βεκχορ y : Βελχορ A : Βεεχορ v : Βαιχεωρ <44> : Βιεχωρ <242> : Βεχθορι <246> |

12:9 Ιαβιν boc₂e₂ b₂] Ιαβις Bya₂ A pqtz efmsw MNaghinvw b₂ : Ιαβης cx : > d(*haplography*) |

14:49 Ιεσσιου bc₂e₂ h] Ιεσσιουλ By : Ιεσσιουδ a₂ : Ιεσιουδ z : Ιεσσηου o : Ιεσσουι Nanb₂ : Ιεσσουι v : Ιεσσου fmsw i : Ιεσου e : Ισουι Acx : Εσουι g : Ιησουι dlpqt : Ιησουε <74> : Ιασουρ <71> : Ιεσους Jos-cod : Ιησους Jos-ed |

19:22 Σεφι boc₂e₂ Ba₂ z(mg¹) i] Σειφι y : Σεφιν efmsw ghᵇ⁷v : Σεφιειν h* : Σεφεειν n : Σεφιην N : Σεφιειμ z(mg) jb₂ : Εφιειμ <71> : Εφειν a : Εσσωφειν Or-gr : Σοχω c dp : Σωχω lqtz(txt) : Σοκχω A : Σογχω x |

24:23 Μεσσαρα boe₂ B z] Μεσσερα c₂ : Μεσιρα g : Μεσσαρ a₂ : Μεσσαραν y b₂ : Μεσσαραμ j : Μεσαρα cᵃ⁷x msw n : Μεσσαραν e : Μεσσαρας A : Μεσερα hᵇ⁷ : Μεσηρα v : Μασαρα f : Μασερα h* : Μεσσηρα c* dlqpt Nai |

26:1 Εχελα boc₂e₂] Χελμαθ Ba₂ : Μελχαο y : Εχελαθ efmsw hᵇ⁷ : Εχελλατ t : Αχιλα Acx : Εχεα v : Εχελατ dlpqz MNagh*ijnb₂ |

26:3 Εχελα boc₂ Bya₂ A h*] Εχελαν e₂ : Εχελαμ a : Εχελατ dlpqtz MNgijvb₂ : Εχελαθ efm*sw hᵇ⁷ : Εχελαχ m* : Εχελαζ <71> : Σικελλα Jos(vid) : Αχιμα cx |

28:4 Σωμαν boc₂e₂ Bya₂ i] Σωμαμ z : Σωναμ dlqptz efmsw MNaghjnb₂ On Cyr Thdt : Σοναμ <44> : Σωνα <71> : Οναμ c v : Γωναμαν A |

29:1 Αφεκ boc₂e₂ Bya₂ Acx] Αφεκα dlpqtz e Ng : Αφεκκα fmsw Ma(vid)hijvb₂ |

31:12 Βαιθσαν boc₂e₂ y ahᵃ⁷] Βαιθσαμ B ptz s MNh*jb₂ : Βεθσαμ dq efw i : Βιθσαμ g : Βεθσαν a₂ vᵇ : Βηθσαν Ax Jos(vid) : Βιθσαν c : Βαιθσαμυς y n |

Nine of these readings have wide variations on the name, seven are B readings, leaving four that have no support from uncial manuscripts so that in these instances Rahlfs accepts readings supported only by minuscules. Certainly this is the case with Ιαβιν in 12:9, and the name

of Saul's son Ιεσσιου in 14:49. The support for the place name Εχελα
in 26:3 by MSS Bya₂ A is probably determinative also in 26:1, rather than
indicating any preference for the reliability of the Lucianic tradition here.

The form of the first proper name in this category–Σηλω (1:9)–is
characteristic of the Lucianic manuscripts.[14] Rahlfs has been misled by
his preference for MS B at this point. In the nine other instances of the
name in 1 Reigns the Old Greek reads Σηλωμ, a reading which is also
shared by the majority of the database manuscripts at 1:9. On the other
hand, in the nine instances where the Old Greek has Σηλωμ the Lucian-
ic text reads Σηλω. By whatever means the reading found its way into
the text of MSS Ba₂, it is the Lucianic reading.

At 31:12 it is clear that Rahlfs has been guided by the MT בית שׁן
to adopt the reading closest to MS B that best reflects the Hebrew, in this
case the Lucianic text. However, by so doing he has rejected the more
difficult reading of MS B in favor of agreement with the Hebrew.[15]

The following three readings are included in the base text (pri-
marily) on the authority of the Lucianic manuscripts:[16]

    14:41 ει boc₂(sub ÷)e₂ lz esw n
    24:1 ανεβη boc₂e₂
    26:18 μου boc₂e₂ cx qᵃ⁷z i

The first word is a letter variant, with the rest of the tradition reading η.
As evidenced by the presence of the hexaplaric obelus (which is correct),

---

[14]The word 'characteristic' is used in this context to indicate that either the same
word, or form of the word, always occurs in the Lucianic manuscripts in contradistinction
to the majority tradition, or, where it is deemed that there are sufficient occurrences to
warrant exceptions, that it usually occurs. In such instances the degree of support and the
exceptions are indicated.

[15]Thus he has not followed his mentor's canon. See p. 33, f.n. 8.

[16]"... included ... on the authority of the Lucianic manuscripts" because Rahlfs lists
them under the siglum 'L' in the apparatus to his text; "... (primarily) ..." because two of
the readings have wider support, although this does not appear to have been a factor with
Rahlfs as indicated by his including them under the Lucianic siglum 'L' alone.

this passage was in Origen's Greek text but not in his Hebrew text.[17] The sequence in the Lucianic text and its supporters is ει ... η: "If ... or," whereas in the rest of the manuscripts it is η ... η: "either ... or." Although the Lucianic reading better suits the context it is notoriously difficult to assess originality with such letter variants.

Driver says of the opening ויעל of 24:1: "Very surprising, in the present context"[18] because the topography of the land was such that it was impossible for David to have 'gone up' to En Gedi from where he was. Perhaps because of this Rahlfs has preferred the conceptually more difficult reading of the Lucianic text which accurately represents the extant Hebrew text over the presumably redactional ανεστη of the rest of the Greek tradition, and which removes the problem.[19]

This reading is important in the larger context of the textual tradition as a whole, because it is but one of over 300 instances in 1 Reigns where the Lucianic manuscripts are either the only ones, or are among a small minority of the other manuscripts, that witness to a Hebrew *Vorlage* closer to the MT than other witnesses. Certainly subsequent research will need to address this issue, especially in the light of so-called 'proto-Lucianic' studies.[20]

Though it is difficult to assign precise weight to manuscript groupings in the third example, with the hexaplaric MSS cx also sharing the reading, it is worthy of note that it does have the support of the

---

[17]It is generally agreed that the first part of this verse (covered by the obelus in MS c₂) is lacking due to haplography (although for an alternative explanation see Tsevat, *IDBS*, p. 778).

[18]Driver, *Notes*, p. 191.

[19]Relative to the Hebrew, the non-Lucianic text is *"lectio difficilior"* (see Lagarde's "rules" p. 33, f.n. 8). Nevertheless Rahlfs chose the reading closer to the Hebrew.

[20]Barthélemy remarks that ". . . D'ailleurs ces modifications qui le rendraient plus fidèle à l'hébreu (par le détour des emprunts qu'il a faits aux hexaples) sont assez négligeables en nombre et en importance" ("Reexamination," p. 70).

Hebrew text, which may have been a factor for Rahlfs. On the other hand, the reading of the Lucianic text is part of a longer reading supported only by manuscripts boc₂e₂ i: ο κυριος μου ο βασιλευς, the last two words of which do not have MT support. It is quite possible that the addition of μου is part of this longer expression, and that the support of the MT is incidental. Nevertheless in this instance Rahlfs has preferred the longer text over the rest of the tradition.[21]

Of the remaining thirty-two readings in which Rahlfs accepts a minority reading supported by Lucianic, three are of special interest. The first attests Atticistic tendencies by reading the Attic contraction of the form νεομηνια:[22]

20:8 νουμηνια boc₂e₂ Bya₂ Njb₂

The next reading presumably dropped out of the rest of the manuscripts due to haplography:

26:10 η *boc₂e₂* B c e ahi

In the sequence εαν μη κυριος παιση αυτον η η ημερα αυτου ελθη only one of the two single η's was written.

In the final example the phrase ανδρα και γυναικα in the sense of "man or[/nor] woman," is replaced in the rest of the tradition by ανδρα η γυναικα (27:9 and 30:2).[23] All of these single readings are isolated examples that do not establish any trends.

---

[21]Ms a₂ includes a μου a few words later, but given the different context in which it is added (it alone has the reading) there is no reason to conclude that it is a transposition of the same pronoun.

[22]See below under Substitutions for further details.

[23]In the latter case MSS lpqtz MNijvb₂ read ουδε for η (or και). Further, in this verse MSS oc₂e₂ alone read και where the others have αλλ' in the sense of "but."

2. multiple word readings

Only three passages occur in this category. The first (9:15: προς αυτον) is paralleled in the majority tradition by a transposition:

```
Rahlfs: εμπροσθεν του ελθειν προς αυτον    Σαουλ
   Maj: εμπροσθεν του ελθειν              Σαουλ προς αυτον
   Luc: εμπροσθεν του ελθειν προς αυτον τον Σαουλ
```

The Lucianic text on the one hand shares the word order accepted by Rahlfs (probably on the basis of MSS By), but on the other hand, in the same context, includes the article along with MSS cx i, possibly to indicate that the indeclinable proper name is in the accusative case, although it could merely be either haplography on the part of MSS By, or dittography (αυτον ... τον) on the part of the Lucianic manuscripts.

When the second passage[24] is taken in its context it is apparent that it is unlikely that the Lucianic text played any significant part in Rahlfs' selection of the reading because of the extended nature of the Lucianic text, and the context of the majority text:

```
   Maj:  και Σαουλ ελαχε του βασιλευειν
Rahlfs:  και Σαουλ                     κατακληρουται
   Luc:  και Σαου                      κατακληρουται

   Maj:                         επι Ισραηλ
Rahlfs:         εργον           επι Ισραηλ
   Luc:  το εργον του βασιλευειν επι Ισραηλ
```

The third example is noted for the curious text that it preserves:

22:7 και ειπεν Σαουλ προς τους παιδας αυτου τους παρεστη-κοτας αυτω και ειπεν αυτοις ....

"And Saul said to his servants that stood by him, (and he said to them) ...."

---

[24] 14:47 κατακληρουται εργον boc₂e₂ B cx z(mg)

In the context, the second και ειπεν αυτοις [+ Σαουλ boc₂] is pleo-
nastic. Rahlfs has apparently concluded that it is original, and while that
is possible, it also could be a doublet, or due to dittography.[25]

2. Omissions

The base text category contained Lucianic readings shared in
common with the Rahlfs text. Omissions and the remaining three
categories–substitutions, transpositions, and additions–record where the
Lucianic text differs from the Rahlfs text.

The omissions category covers several different types of shorter
readings. Virtual transpositions[26] have been removed from omissions
and the corresponding readings transferred from the additions category
to the transpositions category. In addition to these the omissions
category retains shorter readings that combine with substitution or
additions readings in a Lucianic text that does not have a formal
one-to-one equivalence with the base text, such as where a personal
pronoun substitutes for a noun with the article, in which case both a
substitution and an omission are generated. At 6:7 the Old Greek τας
βοας is represented by the Lucianic αυτας, the pronoun standing for the
stated subject. As will be seen when the additions category is studied,
the Lucianic text is often the reverse, where pronouns are replaced by
nouns–especially proper nouns–to clarify subjects or objects.

What remains after all these adjustments have been made is a
group of shorter readings that potentially fall into one of two categories:
those that bear witness to pre-Lucianic recensional activity, and those
that are the result of the work of Lucian himself. Unfortunately there is
no ready way to confidently distinguish one from the other, so they are
studied together.

---

[25]The phrase is not found in the MT.

[26]See pp. 25-26.

a. statistical analysis

Table 9

Lucianic Majority Omissions of the Base Text

boc_2e_2	350	$b\ c_2e_2$	6
boc_2	4	oc_2e_2	7
$bo\ e_2$	5		

Total: 372

Table 10

Non-Lucianic Support for Lucianic Majority Omissions

b	365	B	3	d	75	e	10	M	0
o	366	y	22	l	7	f	13	N	12
c_2	367	a_2	50	p	21	m	10	a	39
e_2	368			q	12	s	15	g	47
				t	16	w	7	h	43
				z	35			i	65
		A	31					j	4
		c	82					n	11
		x	90					v	40
								b_2	9

Clearly the Lucianic manuscripts constitute a family. Of the non-Lucianic manuscripts, MSS cx are the closest to the Lucianic, and independent of MS A, although at the same time they share less than one quarter of the Lucianic readings. Standing out among the rest is MS d, a relation not seen in the base text statistics, and in fact caution is justified in this connection because MS d omits so much in general that it can rightly be termed 'abbreviating.'[27]

---

[27]Ulrich calls MS d "... the peculiar and abbreviating MS ...." In his study of the Old Latin he found that one of the ancestors of this manuscript sometimes bridges between the Latin and the Hebrew, and he observes that the manuscript "deserves special study ..." ("The Old Latin Translation of the LXX and the Hebrew Scrolls from Qumran," Emanuel Tov, ed, *HGTS*, p. 154). In the light of the degree of abbreviation in MS d, it is possible that a study of it may be able to throw some light on the situation in Job and Jeremiah

It needs to be kept in mind that, due to the somewhat artificial divisions created by the categories, it is possible to have chance agreements between manuscripts in one or a few categories for reasons other than family relationships. This is especially true in the omissions category where coincidental factors combine to create an artificial picture of closeness that is not sustained in other categories.

b. synoptic survey of omissions

Table 11

Omissions Range of Variants

Adjectives	11	Names	18	Preposit's	57
Adverbs	16	Nouns	30	Pronouns	44
Articles	71	Numbers	4	Translit's	2
Conjunct's	71	Particles	23	Verbs	23
Interject's	2				

The prominent types of words "omitted" here are articles, conjunctions, prepositions, and pronouns.

1. single word readings

In 1:23 and 8:6 εν οφθαλμοις is represented in Lucian by the koine word ενωπιον.[28] 17 of the 57 omissions passages in which the Lucianic text lacks a preposition concern the preposition εν.

Two of these, 7:10 and 30:3, express the instrument by the classical Greek simple dative rather than the koine εν with the dative. In a different context the simple dative is preferred in 20:19 to express "time at which," while in 25:37 "his heart died within him" is expressed by Lucian as (literally): "his heart died to him" (no expressed preposition)." Finally,

---

where a shorter text, or an abbreviated text, is a central issue.

[28]Thackeray says " ... ενωπιον which is unknown to the classical language, but is found in the papyri from ii/-i/ B.C. onwards, is a favorite rendering of לפני and בעיני" (*Grammar*, p. 42).

in four instances (14:36, 23:2, and 23:5 [twice]) εν with the dative to express the partitive is represented by the simple accusative. In the first of these the difference is as follows:

Maj: και διαρπασωμεν εν αυτοις
Luc: και διαρπασωμεν   αυτους

with Lucian reading "plunder" rather than the Old Greek partitive "plunder among." Similarly, in the second instance the command in the Lucianic text is to "smite the Philistines" rather than (literally) to "smite among the Philistines," implying that it was from the outset only to be partial.

Martin says that εν is "the most frequently used preposition in translation Greek ..."[29] and that "the use of the dative case, other than its use as the object of *en*" is a syntactical feature which is "*less frequent* in Greek which is a translation of Hebrew or Aramaic than in original Greek prose writings."[30] If Martin is correct, then both of these changes make the Lucianic text look less like a translation, although the use of ενωπιον to represent εν οφθαλμοις is less clear because the improper preposition, while the neuter of the adjective ενωπιος is etymologically a compound of εν.

Of the seventy-one conjunctions that are not shared by the Lucianic manuscripts thirty-four are the word και. As a rule this conjunction occurs more frequently in Greek translated from a Semitic source than in a work written in Greek due to parataxis in the source.

The absence of these conjunctions in Lucian can be accounted for in two ways. It can be argued that the Old Greek was faithful to the

---

[29]R.A. Martin, "Some Syntactical Criteria of Translation Greek," *VT* 10 (1960), p. 295.

[30]Idem, "Syntax Criticism of the LXX Additions to the Book of Esther" (*JBL* 94 [1975], p. 65). See also his *Syntactical Evidence of Semitic Sources in Greek Documents* (SBL Septuagint and Cognate Studies, 3; Missoula: Scholars Press, 1974) pp. 5-38.

Hebrew text in including these conjunctions, but that the Lucianic text has omitted them to remove one of the obvious marks of translation. On the other hand, however, the application of Lagarde's "rules" requires that readings which are less like the Hebrew and less literal be adopted as those most likely to reflect the original text, which in this case would be the Lucianic text. It seems as though the relation to the Hebrew was determinative for Rahlfs.

At 1:20 it appears that the conjunction has been edited out:[31]

Maj: και εκαλεσεν το ονομα αυτου Σαμουηλ και ειπεν οτι
Luc: και εκαλεσεν το ονομα αυτου Σαμουηλ   λεγουσα

In 3:19 (and *passim*) it appears that the word is simply omitted. One senses as these are studied, one after another, that the result is usually to move away from the slavishly literal flavor of the Old Greek text.

In some of the passages the editor's red ink can almost be seen as passages are reworded to express the ideas better. In a number of instances unnecessary repetitions are avoided: 8:2 ονομα ... ονομα only once, 8:13 εις ... εις ... εις only once, and similarly the multiple prepositions at 10:1, 12:5, 13:22, 17:9, and 18:4 occur only once in the Lucianic text.

The editor can also be seen at work in 15:23:

Maj: οτι   εξουδενωσας το ρημα κυριου και εξουδενωσει
Luc: ανθ' ων εξουδενωσας το ρημα κυριου   εξουδενωσει

Maj: σε κυριος   μη ειναι βασιλεα επι Ισραηλ.
Luc: σε κυριος του μη βασιλευειν   επι Ισραηλ.

The meaning is essentially the same in each text, but the manner of expressing it is different.

---

[31]See also 11:11, 14:43, 25:23.

One of the general characteristics of the Lucianic text is the frequent inclusion of the article.[32] Thus it is interesting that some seventy-one times the Lucianic manuscripts do not include the article. Some of these were with articular infinitives, some are omitted when a noun is replaced by a pronoun, some are omitted with proper names, while others are omitted when a person or event is introduced for the first time.

There are two trends that warrant mention. Seven times the particle δη is omitted, although it still occurs some thirty-six times in the Lucianic majority text. Three times σημερον occurs with ημερα (12:5, 17:10 σημερον εν ταυτη (τη) ημερα, 29:6 σημερον ημερας), but in each of these Lucian omits σημερον.

2. multiple word readings

One of the most striking features of these readings is that if one were to switch the omissions sign to an additions sign in the list of the multiple readings, it would not be possible to detect the change, because the readings omitted are of the same character as those added.

Some of the readings remove apparent doublets found in the base text (2:24, 12:4, 20:25, 20:42, and 24:16). This is important to note because one of the frequently claimed characteristics of the Lucianic text is the presence of doublets. There are in fact numerous doublets, but the situation is not as simple as merely adding the Lucianic readings to the Old Greek text: there are doublets shared by the Old Greek and the Lucianic text that presumably originate from the Old Greek,[33] there are

---

[32]For details see below under Additions.

[33]Twenty-five Old Greek doublets were isolated in the course of the research on the first twenty-one chapters: 1:3, 1:11, 1:26, 2:16, 2:24, 4:14, 5:4 (*bis*), 5:12, 6:8, 6:11, 6:15, 7:12, 12:5, 14:4 (*bis*), 14:25, 15:8, 15:17, 17:10, 20:35, 21:3, 21:8, 21:14.

doublets in the Old Greek that are not in the Lucianic text (as here), and there are doublets in the Lucianic text that are not in the Old Greek.[34]

In addition, repetitious readings (as opposed to formal doublets) have also been removed in 14:42, 16:18, 17:22, 20:37, 20:40 and 23:6. The substitution of ουτως for the Old Greek κατα το ρημα τουτο (17:30) is a classic editorial improvement.

3. Substitutions

This group of variants is the largest studied so far, and the second largest single category (after additions) among the Lucianic majority variants. It is appropriate then to consider their implications. First, Brock has demonstrated that however much the Lucianic text may owe to its *Vorlage*, the text as it exists in the manuscripts has been stamped by Lucian's fourth century work.[35] Second, this work was recensional and not a fresh translation. Third, there is no way of establishing within the parameters of this synchronic study whether individual readings differ because of the fourth century editing, or whether they were already in the *Vorlage* of the Lucianic text, or whether they crept into the text through harmonization to the majority text in the subsequent years down to the tenth century, the earliest date for the existing Lucianic manuscripts. Readings that were already in the *Vorlage* have been detected by comparison with texts such as the Qumran material and the Old Latin. However this evidence is at best fragmentary and only proves useful where the reference text is extant, because the early readings isolated by this

---

[34]Thirty-six Lucianic doublets were isolated during the course of the study, although the list is not exhaustive: 1:3 (*not the same as Old Greek*), 1:5, 1:6, 1:7, 1:16, 1:17, 1:20, 1:25, 2:2, 2:21, 2:30, 2:32, 2:34, 3:6, 4:18, 6:5, 6:12, 9:9, 10:27/11:1, 11:5, 12:3, 13:2, 13:15, 14:40, 15:3, 15:23, 15:29, 15:32, 16:20, 17:2, 20:35, 21:3 (*not the same as Old Greek*), 21:27, 29:3, 29:10, 30:19.

[35]He says "If it was not Lucian himself, then it was an Antiochene contemporary of his who put the final form on the 'Lucianic' text as we know it to-day" ("Recensions," "Abstract" p. 6).

means are usually not of such a character as to be identifiable in those places where the text is not extant.

Fourth, the majority of the Lucianic characteristics are found within this category. From these characteristics Brock selected the four most clear-cut, and described them as follows:[36]

> i. ἅλως masc: regularly corrected by L[ucian] to fem.
>
> ii. ἔλεος neuter, 3rd decl.: regularly corrected in the oblique cases by L to masc. 2nd decl.[37]
>
> iii. εἶπα and all Ist aorist forms (except εἴπατε, εἰπάτωσαν: εἶπας and the infin. do not occur in I Kms) regularly corrected by L to 2nd aorist.
>
> iv. aor. pass. of γίνομαι altered to middle in L in all cases but four.[38]

He goes on to observe:

> These alterations can be regarded as the hall-mark of the 'Lucianic' recension, and can in turn be used as a criterion for isolating 'Lucianic' mss in books where these are not yet clearly defined.

a. statistical analysis

The decision to hold the minimum number of non-Lucianic manuscripts to six in determining which variants to use for analysis, while serving its original purpose of limiting the amount of data for consideration, does create sharper distinctions among the manuscripts than would be the case if more manuscripts were admitted.

---

[36]"Recensions," p. 265. The comments are his.

[37]There are five examples (Brock lists four, omitting the last): 14:45, 15:6, 20:8, 14, 15.

[38]There are in fact five exceptions: 4:7, 10:27, 18:10, 30:1, 31:8.

Table 12

Lucianic Readings Substituted for the Base Text

boc_2e_2	1100	$b\ c_2e_2$	78
boc_2	43	oc_2e_2	63
$bo\ \ e_2$	19		

Total: 1303

Table 13

Non-Lucianic Support for Lucianic Majority Substitutions

b	1240	B	10	d	66	e	44	M	2
o	1225	y	35	l	8	f	61	N	23
c_2	1284	a_2	69	p	47	m	28	a	35
e_2	1260			q	34	s	42	g	107
				t	37	w	37	h	74
				z	121			i	130
		A	30					j	10
		c	76					n	16
		x	76					v	66
								b_2	22

Within the Lucianic manuscripts themselves there is the expected high degree of affinity. Ms o is the most independent, but that concerns only a small fraction of the total readings. The manuscripts closest to the Lucianic group in each of the categories studied so far have shared only about 10% of the Lucianic variants. This was not anticipated from the initial collations for Chapter Two, where the statistics from all of the manuscripts in the database were compiled.[39] In that case a figure of 10% often represented the manuscripts furthest from the collation manuscript, and figures such as 30-40% represented the manuscripts outside of the collation family that showed affinity.

The highest non-Lucianic figures here are for MSS ghiz. While manuscripts that share similar statistics need not bear any relation to

---

[39]See the Appendix.

each other, especially when each shares only 10%, in this case they do relate to each other. In 1 Reigns 17 there is a repetitiveness to the pattern of MSS bghiozc₂e₂ sharing readings together that is not reflected elsewhere.[40] Thus though the Lucianic manuscripts have these hexaplaric passages, there is often an independence from MS A, but an affinity with MSS ghi.

Next in frequency are MSS cx which are again closer than MS A, and show a definite, if distant relationship.

In this category the data is now free of the direct influence of both MS B and MS A in the manner seen in the base text and omissions categories. In fact it is possible to see why the Lucianic manuscripts do not share the base text readings, and what it is that makes them distinctive.

b. synoptic survey

In the base text and omissions categories, as will be the case with transpositions and additions, there is essentially no point of comparison, so the synopsis simply lists the types of variants involved. Here, however, there is a direct point of comparison: the base text. Consequently it is possible to provide more comprehensive statistics for substitutions.

Table 14

Substitutions Range of Variants

Adjectives	44	Names	79	Preposit's	92
Same	23	Same	0	Same	0
Synon.	17	Synon.	45	Synon.	78
Diff.	4	Diff.	34	Diff.	14
Adverbs	23	Nouns	211	Pronouns	90
Same	0	Same	91	Same	55
Synon.	14	Synon.	67	Synon.	13
Diff.	9	Diff.	53	Diff.	22

---

[40]However, a relationship–even if more distant–does exist outside of the hexaplaric passages.

Table 14 cont.

Articles	115	Numbers	4	Translit's	2
Same	106	Same	0	Same	0
Synon.	1	Synon.	0	Synon.	0
Diff.	8	Diff.	4	Diff.	0
Conjunct's	30	Particip's	42	Verbs	375
Same	0	Same	28	Same	196
Synon.	14	Synon.	9	Synon.	131
Diff.	16	Diff.	5	Diff.	48
Interject's	2	Particles	23	Inner-Gr.	171
Same	0	Same	0		
Synon.	0	Synon.	15		
Diff.	2	Diff.	8		

The part of speech most affected by this type of variant is the verb. The above table shows verbs substituted 375 times, but this time there is also a separate list for participles[41] which contains an additional 42 words, giving a total of some 32% of all these variants. Of these verbs, only 48 (15.3%) are different words, the rest being either the same word or a synonym of it.

There are some 211 variants among the nouns, almost half of which are synonyms. In the case of proper nouns there are 64 variants, 42 of which are spelling variants.[42] With both of these–nouns and names–where they replace a pronoun they are listed under 'different,' and vice versa where pronouns replace either nouns or names.

Next in frequency are the inner Greek variants. These include spelling variants, alternate forms (either required or suggested by the context, such as ἐμοῦ and μου, and οὐ/οὐκ/οὐχ), as well as the inevi-

---

[41]This was done so that the morphological analysis, not included here, that was done for each variant in this category could also nuance the noun-type features of the participle.

[42]There are no occurrences where the same word is a majority variant even though some of the proper names do decline.

table letter variant confusions between such forms as υμιν and ημιν.[43] Then there are interchanges such as μεσσαβ and υποστασεως (14:12), and Συρος and Ιδουμαιος (21:8).

Articles and pronouns have high percentages of original readings because the changes are mainly of such things as case, number, gender, etc. The eight 'different' readings for the definite articles are due to data entry level decisions that substituted articles for other parts of speech, such as την (Γεθθαιους) for αυτην (5:9), and οι for ουκ (5:12).[44]

1. single word readings

This category contains the highest number of characteristic readings. Because the interest here is synopsis, only characteristics in addition to those listed above from Brock are included.

a. The Lucianic manuscripts have Ακχους for the Old Greek Αγχους (= MT אכיש). This occurs 21 times in chapters 21, 27-28 and 29, is consistent, and confined solely to the Lucianic manuscripts.

b. The formula: το αρεστον ενωπιον. . .
                 το αρεστον εν οφθαλμοις. . .

occurs each time for the Old Greek:

                 το αγαθον ενωπιον. . .
                 το αγαθον εν οφθαλμοις. . .

The use of αρεστον (not αγαθον) is characteristic of Lucian, with a few other manuscripts sharing some of the readings (MSS dpqtz share the first one in chapter one), although none consistently share the pattern. Although it occurs only six times (1:23, 3:18, 11:10, 14:36, 40, 24:5) it is included because it occurs consistently.

---

[43]The majority text is relatively free of this type of variant, although, as will be seen when the minority variants are studied, this is not the case with the minority readings.

[44]Were the data to be arranged differently these would then appear as plusses.

c. Ενωπιον occurs some 72 times in Lucian, four times replacing εν
οφθαλμοις (which occurs 19 times in Lucian), although by far the
majority of the instances were inherited from its ancestor.[45] As noted
above, ενωπιον is a *koine* word.   While more classical forms are
occasionally used (as noted below), *koine* words are also substituted.

d. For the Old Greek: εχθες και τριτην [ημερας]

        Lucian reads: εχθες και τριτης [ημερας]

This is formulaic in this context.[46]

Four times it is either unique to Lucian, or else in a very small
minority; once it is shared with MSS A dpqtz; and once it is shared by the
majority, with only MSS BNcefhns reading τριτην.[47]

e. From 17:39 onwards through the end of 1 Reigns the Lucianic manu-
scripts have μαχαιρα ten times in place of the Old Greek ρομφαια,
although in the same section they do have ρομφαια nine times as well
(out of a total of sixteen for the whole book). All except one of the ten
occurrences of μαχαιρα are (essentially) unique to Lucian. Ms B does
not have it at all, and MS A has it only at 25:13 twice.

These readings are important because they are (essentially)
confined to Lucian, but lack overall consistency. If it were known that
the Lucianic text as it exists was in the same form as it was when it left
the redactor's hand around the fourth century, then it would be clear that
the presence of both these words was due to partial redaction.

_____

[45]That is to say they are shared in common with the majority of the non-Lucianic
manuscripts.

[46]Τριτην does not occur in this context in Lucian.

[47]Conybeare and Stock (*A Grammar of Septuagint Greek*, # 86 pp. 78-79) list the
various forms of this expression in the LXX, none of which includes τριτης in 1-3 Reigns,
but there is one occurrence in 4 Reigns 13:5.

On the contrary, all that is available today is the witness borne by manuscript copies that are removed by more than six to ten centuries from the original editing. During that time the manuscripts were exposed to various hazards, including harmonization to the majority text, a phenomenon which could equally account for the presence of both μαχαιρα and ρομφαια as the theory of partial editing in the fourth century.

f. Similar to the above type of reading is the Lucianic use of διοτι. It is found eighteen times in the Lucianic text, of which two are shared by the majority of all the manuscripts, one has no direct equivalent in the majority, and the remaining fifteen are found where the Old Greek has οτι and are (essentially) unique to Lucian.[48] Euphony does not seem to be a factor in its use, and it leaves 215 occurrences of οτι in the Lucianic text.[49]

g. The Attic contraction νουμηνια occurs three times in the Lucianic text (20:5, 18, 24) in connection with Saul's new moon feast. Twice it corresponds to the Old Greek νεομηνια, and once to μην. Thus the Lucianic text is consistent in the form it uses.

h. When the augment is used with προφητευω in the Lucianic manuscripts it is always added in the more classical form between the prefix and the verb: προεφητευσεν for the Old Greek επροφητευσεν.

---

[48]The total in MS B is five, and in MS A six.

[49]Thackeray comments (*Grammar*, p. 138, # 12): "Hiatus and the harsh juxtaposition of consonants at the close of one word and the beginning of the next were avoided by followers of the rules of Isocrates by the use of some alternative forms. Πᾶς and ἅπας, ὅτι and διότι are the chief examples. In the LXX, as in the Ptolemaic papyri, the employment of ἅπας appears to be due in most books to regard for euphony, whereas διότι is used indiscriminately after vowels and consonants."

i. Except at 1:3,[50] the Lucianic text consistently reads Σηλω for the ten occurrences of Σηλωμ in the Old Greek.[51]

j. The Lucianic majority text reads Σεκελαγ for the Old Greek Σεκελακ.[52]

In addition to these, other readings are worthy of note since they occur relatively frequently but fall short of being clear-cut characteristics.

The first such example is the use of δε in place of και. The Lucianic majority text has δε 39 times, 15 of which are shared with the Old Greek text. In chapter one alone it occurs seven times.[53] Some of these instances, such as the first occurrence (1:2), have a genuine contrastive element; in 1:18 the definite article is also added as a case and gender marker to identify the subject of the verb ειπεν; but in general

---

[50]In this case it would seem that the exception is rather due to contamination than to inconsistent or partial redaction.

[51]This is true despite the variant form Ηλω listed by B-M for MS b (4:12) which is in fact due to haplography: εις Ηλω < εις Σηλω.

[52]26:4 (την ερημον e₂), 27:6 (*first time* Σεκελακ o, *second time* Σελαγ e₂), 30:1 (*three times, first time* Σικελαγ b), 30:3, 30:14 (Σελαγ o), 30:26.

[53]The spread of its occurrence in the Lucianic text is informative:

chapter	times	chapter	times
1	7	17	3
2	2	18	1
3	1	19	1
7	1	20	2
9	2	24	2
10	1	25	2
12	2	26	2
13	2	28	1
15	2	30	4
16	1		

If the rate of inclusion in chapter one had been maintained throughout, the complexion of the recension would be quite different in this respect.

there is no evident reason for the preference, and usage is similar to that in the NT.

In the Lucianic text as it exists today there is a partial substitution of πεδιον for the Old Greek αγρος. Twice Lucian reads πεδιον with the Old Greek, but in six of the twenty Old Greek occurrences of αγρος, Lucian reads πεδιον.[54] There are no clear-cut differences that distinguish the two readings except that πεδιον is always with the article while αγρος has it only once (8:14).

The treatment of the names Γαβεε and Γαβαα is informative. In the five occurrences of the former in the Old Greek, Lucianic substitutes the latter,[55] and for the four Old Greek occurrences of the latter Lucian uses a form of βουνος[56] except that in one occurrence of Γαβαα (13:15) Lucian retains it and adds βουνον as a doublet.[57]

In a different vein is the presence of thirteen readings of the adverb πλην used as a conjunction, four of which are Lucianic substitutions. Abbott-Smith records Blass as saying of this word that "it is obvious that πλην was the regular word in the vulgar language."[58] The Atticising trend of the Lucianic text has often been highlighted by scholars, but the partial nature of this characteristic can be seen when readings such as πλην, a *koine* word, are not only tolerated but are used as substitutions.

---

[54]Αγρος: 6:14, 18; 8:14; 11:5; 13:17; 19:3; 20:11 (*bis*); 22:7; 25:15; 27:5, 7, 11; 30:11; πεδιον: Old Greek. 14:14; 20:5; Luc. 4:2; 6:1; 14:14, 15; 20:5, 12, 24, 35.

[55]13:2, 13:16, 18; 14:5, 16.

[56]10:26; 11:4; 13:15; 15:34.

[57]Maj: εις γαβαα   Βενιαμιν
   Luc: εις γαβαα βουνον Βενιαμιν

MS c₂ has the phrase under an obelus (÷).

[58]Abbott-Smith, *Lexicon*, p. 365.

One of the features listed for the καίγε text in 2 Reigns is the replacement of the historic presents by a past tense. In the light of this, statistics for the tense changes of the finite verbs were compiled.

Table 15

Substitutions Tense Changes

pres for aor	11
aor for pres	31
impf for aor	9
pres for impf	1
aor for impf	4

Six of the imperfects replacing aorists are in chapter seventeen. While the majority of the changes are to remove historic presents other significant changes occur, especially the counter-move that replaces aorists with present tenses.

The final trend concerns the adjective πας. This word occurs 194 times in the Lucianic majority text, and of these, ten are editorial changes, and 32 are (from the perspective of the Old Greek) added to the text in a manner that can best be described as making passages more comprehensive and inclusive in scope.

2. multiple word readings

Of the multiple word variants 140 are double, 25 are triple, 17 have four words, leaving only five examples that have five or more words. Within this group there are no new characteristics although they do witness to readings such as: αρεστον, αγαθον, Σηλω, εγενετο (and other Attic forms), διοτι, εμε, Γαβαα, νουμηνια, and τριτης ημερας, the significance of all of which has already been noted.

While the focus has been upon the substitutions, this category is also the division of the database that comes closest to the underlying Old Greek text both because it has such a large number of variants, and also because there is not (by definition) a reordering of the text such as is seen in omissions, transpositions, and additions.[59] It is appropriate then to comment here on a characteristic of the Lucianic text shared in common with all of the Old Greek tradition, especially in the light of a statement made under the base text category. It was noted there that over 300 times Lucian shares the MT reading either alone or with a very small minority of the rest of the manuscripts.

As true as that is, and as much as these agreements need to be studied further, they are only one part of the picture. Many passages, some of them extensive in the Old Greek tradition, are not in the MT.[60] These passages bear the hallmarks of translation Greek witnessing to such Semitic syntax as the preposition with the infinitive construct, the infinitive absolute with the finite verb, and parataxis, which are not characteristics of good–or at least standard–Greek style. Clearly such readings witness to a text longer than that preserved in the MT. Thus there are different levels of research in the LXX tradition at large and the Lucianic text in particular. This matter of the comparison of the ancestor of the Greek texts with the MT is at a level deeper than is reached by studying the variants, and is beyond the scope of this study, although the research has been sensitive to its existence.

4. Transpositions

This category combines the essence of both the base text and the substitutions categories–of base text because the majority of the readings are the same as the Old Greek, of substitutions because the remainder are variants to the base text. The difference is that the word order is not the same as the base text.

---

[59]The base text category is similar to the substitutions category in also maintaining the same order and additionally, the same text.

[60]From this it can be seen why it is said that the text of Samuel has suffered from haplography. As Tsevat has pointed out, "Although Samuel has the reputation that its text is among the worst of the OT books, this is not evident to the ordinary reader" ("Samuel, I and II," *IDBS*, p. 777). It is chiefly discerned by comparison with a fuller text.

a. statistical analysis

Table 16

Lucianic Majority Transpositions of the Base Text

boc_2e_2	386	$b\ c_2e_2$	11
boc_2	2	oc_2e_2	3
$bo\ e_2$	7		

Total: 409

Table 17

Non-Lucianic Support for Lucianic Majority Transpositions

b	406	B	0	d	20	e	2	M	3
o	398	y	6	l	2	f	8	N	1
c_2	402	a_2	18	p	19	m	5	a	3
e_2	407			q	2	s	3	g	25
				t	2	w	3	h	48
				z	41			i	27
		A	29					j	4
		c	29					n	4
		x	26					v	11
								b_2	1

It is clear that again a high degree of agreement exists among the Lucianic manuscripts with only 23 majority variants not shared by all of these manuscripts. This results in a difference of only 9 between the highest (MS e_2) and the lowest (MS o).

The closest to the Lucianic family is MS h at approximately 12%, followed by MS z at approximately 10% then MSS gi at close to 5%. By now this is a familiar ring inasmuch as they have been noted above as sharing both hexaplaric and non-hexaplaric material with the Lucianic manuscripts to this (limited) extent. The continued presence of these manuscripts in readings that have been selected solely because they are (distinctly) Lucianic, indicates that there is a distant relationship, though not affinity.

The above statistics for the A family, and especially those of MS A, witness to transpositions outside of the hexaplaric passages, because in the hexaplaric passages the A text is the base text. In Chapter Two it was noted that the Lucianic manuscripts share 30-35% of the A (non-hexaplaric) transposition readings, and it is some of these readings that are in evidence here.

b. synoptic survey

No list of the parts of speech for this category can be furnished because, as noted in Chapter One, the selection of which variants to tag as being transposed is an arbitrary decision, and for this database was motivated by the desire to have transpositions follow their omissions reference where possible, rather than vice versa.[61]

1. single word readings[62]

Although the order of the elements of a Greek sentence[63] is more flexible than it is in an English sentence, there are patterns that are characteristic of the language, and patterns that are characteristic of a writer. One of the interests, then, as this section was studied, was to attempt to ascertain in what way the inverted word order altered the nature of the text. It was anticipated when this study was first undertaken that where the changes could be defined in terms of style (and not all can be) they would be towards a 'better' Greek style. Though some can be so described, others are best described as moving in the opposite direction.

---

[61]See pp. 25-26.

[62]In the context of transpositions the word 'single' is used to refer to the element of the altered word order that is tagged in the database as a transposition.

[63]These include such parts of the sentence as subject, object, verb, etc.

Some of those which move towards a better Greek style, especially in the sense of a less Semitic style are:

4:11
    Maj: και αμφοτεροι οι υιοι Ηλι απεθανον Οφνι και Φινεες
    Luc: και αμφοτεροι οι υιοι Ηλι   Οφνι και Φινεες απεθανον

Here the verb follows the subject, as seems preferable in original Greek.

11:11
    Maj: και εισπορευονται εις μεσον της παρεμβολης
    Luc: και εισπορευονται εις μεσον της παρεμβολης

    Maj: εν φυλακη τη πρωεινη
    Luc: των υιων Αμμων εν   τη πρωεινη φυλακη

The section of primary interest here is the better style achieved by the order εν τη πρωεινη φυλακη, although the example also includes a Lucianic anticipatory addition that names the sons of Ammon ahead of the Old Greek.

23:26
    Maj: και ην Δαυιδ   σκεπαζομενος
    Luc: και   Δαυιδ ην σκεπαζομενος

25:1
    Maj: και απεθανεν Σαμουηλ   και συναθροιζονται
    Luc: και   Σαμουηλ απεθανεν και συναθροιζεται

4:13
    Maj: και   ηλθεν και ιδου
    Luc: και οτε ηλθεν

7:16
    Maj: κατ᾽ ενιαυτον   ενιαυτον
    Luc: ενιαυτον κατ᾽ ενιαυτον[64]

---

[64]Other examples are found in 2:28 εμοι, 3:21 εις προφητην (*this is also a 'virtual transposition'*), 9:21 ανδρος, 12:7 την, 18:30 συνηκεν, 19:9 παρα θεου, and 21:12 εξηρχον.

Though these are the best examples, they are no more than occasional examples that are not sufficient to be definitive. Instead they can best be described as minor editorial changes–certainly the overall nature of the text is not markedly altered. This is especially true since a similar number of examples can be cited that show precisely the opposite trend towards a semitic style:

9:5

Maj: και Σαουλ ειπεν   τω παιδαριω αυτου
Luc: και   ειπεν Σαουλ τω παιδαριω αυτου[65]

10:14

Maj: και ειπεν   ο οικειος αυτου προς αυτον
Luc: και λεγει αυτω ο οικειος αυτου

Here the virtual transposition αυτω replaces προς αυτον and moves the indirect object to a position immediately after the verb in Semitic style.[66]

Some of the transpositions alter the meaning of the text:

2:11

Maj: και το παιδαριον   ην λειτουργων τω προσωπω
Luc: και το παιδαριον Σαμουηλ ην λειτουργων τω

Maj: κυριου   ενωπιον   Ηλι του ιερεως
Luc: κυριω προ προσωπου Ηλι του ιερεως

The Lucianic text, with Samuel ministering for the Lord before Eli, is more precise than the majority text.[67]

---

[65]Similarly 9:27, 12:22, 16:1, 18:8, 19:8, and 24:4.

[66]For similar repositioning of the pronoun as indirect object see also 4:16 (*bis*), (*cf. 4:17 where the Lucianic text adds the pronoun*), 13:14, and 18:17.

[67]The text also contains an explanatory addition which identifies Samuel clearly, although there is really no confusion without it. This type of addition will be seen to be common in the Lucianic text.

The final example concerns the expression εγω ειμι which occurs some nine times[68] in the majority text. In three of these instances (17:43, 18:18 and 30:13) the order in Lucian is reversed to read ειμι εγω. This is of interest because of its characteristic–even if unusual–use in the βδ passages. It is clear that the use has no regular pattern in 1 Reigns.

2. multiple word readings

The majority of the transposition multiple readings are in groups of two or three.[69] The breakdown is as follows:

Table 18

Transpositions Multiple Word Readings

no. in group	total
2	48
3	23
4	14
5	4
6+	6

In general they conform to the same patterns noted above for the single word readings. Beyond that one question in particular arises in connection with these readings: Is the word order of the transposed readings the same as the MT or not?

To help address this question the readings have been classified three ways:

not in MT	9
MT order	14
not MT order	72

---

[68] 1:15; 4:16; 9:19, 21; 17:8, 43; 18:18; 22:22 and 30:13.

[69] As noted above for 'single' readings, the numbers for the readings in the table are not the total count, but are based on the physical rearrangement in the database. In all instances there is at least one other word involved in the transposition that has not been counted.

The first figure indicates that nine of the transpositions are not in the MT.[70] The second figure indicates the number of readings that are shared with the MT in the transposed (Lucianic) position,[71] while the last records the number of readings that are in the MT but not in the transposed position of the Lucianic text. Thus in the overwhelming majority of cases, though the readings are shared by the MT, they are not in the MT order in the Lucianic text. In 3:17 the lengthy passage ταδε-ρημα rearranges the text so that the *protasis* precedes the *apodosis*; in 17:24 και-αυτου the men fear before they flee; in 18:5 και-Σαουλ David acts as Saul's officer only after he has been appointed; and in 26:1 εκ-Σαουλ, part of the passage is not in the MT, and what is in it is not in the same order.

What then is the common denominator for all these disparate elements? It cannot be the MT because the examples that appear to relate to that are clearly in the minority, but more importantly an alternative explanation lies closer at hand that goes a long way towards accounting for the phenomenon. In general the editing of the Old Greek text over a period of time as a Greek text, even though the resulting redaction was only partial, is sufficient to account for these examples.[72]

---

[70] 2:24 ποιειτε ουτως, 7:9 συν-λαω, 9:12 τα κορασια, 13:11 ως διεταξας, 13:15 εκ Γαλγαλων (*these are only two words in an extended passage lacking in the MT*), 20:9 εις σου, 20:35 καθως εταξατο (*this is the transposition of an Old Greek doublet that MT has only once*), 26:1 εκ αυχμωδους, 26:16 τον βασιλεα.

[71] 2:1 επ' εχθρους, 2:21 και ετεκεν, 5:6 και-αυτης (*this is the closest reading to the MT, although it is not exact, and at the same time is transposed from v. 3*), 12:12 οτι αλλ' η, 17:9 μετ' εμου, 27:7 και εκατονταρχους, 23:14 εν-ερημω, 24:17 τα-ταυτα, 25:41 επι-γην, 26:16 το-υδατος, 27:8 η γη, 28:20 και-νυκτα, 30:19 και-σκυλων, 30:22 και λοιμος.

[72] Not all of these readings are due to editing. Some have a basis in Hebrew variants but there are no criteria that enable one to extrapolate beyond the few examples that are adduced by comparison with such texts as the Qumran fragments. See for instance Ulrich, *Qumran*, pp. 95-118.

5. Additions

This final majority category primarily records the readings in Lucian that are longer than the Old Greek text.

a. statistical analysis

Table 19

Lucianic Majority Additions

boc_2e_2	1231	$b\ c_2e_2$	98
boc_2	39	oc_2e_2	31
$bo\ e_2$	39		

Total: 1438

Table 20

Non-Lucianic Support for Lucianic Majority Additions

b	1407	B	0	d	88	e	46	M	7
o	1340	y	14	l	10	f	42	N	59
c_2	1399	a_2	55	p	90	m	30	a	16
e_2	1399			q	39	s	32	g	261
				t	38	w	54	h	258
				z	394			i	201
		A	107					j	8
		c	115					n	26
		x	121					v	39
								b_2	19

This is the largest group of variants and indicates that the Lucianic text is significantly longer than the Old Greek. Of the Lucianic manuscripts, MS o has the lowest number of readings and MS b the highest.

One of the sources, although by no means the only source of these readings, is the hexaplaric material in chapters 17-18.[73] In Chapter Two

---

[73]None of the readings are from the passage in 13:1 where the Lucianic variants are confined exclusively to the base text category, or from 23:12 where there are no Lucianic variants to the hexaplaric text of MS A and congeners.

it was seen that MSS boc_2e_2 all share virtually the same percentage of the A readings, and it was remarked there that though MS c_2 is the best witness to the hexaplaric signs it is not to be assumed therefrom that it is the best witness to the hexaplaric text. To find here then that MS c_2 has the highest number of readings is to recognize that these totals are not solely (or even necessarily primarily) the hexaplaric readings.

The closest of the non-Lucianic manuscripts is MS z, followed by MSS ghi. While these patterns are by now familiar, there is no sense in which these relative statistical proximities to MSS boc_2e_2 are strong enough to identify them as Lucianic or sub-Lucianic.

The fact that MSS Acx are low is an important indicator that the additions are not just straight hexaplaric readings[74] because around 45% of the readings of MS A were shared by the Lucianic manuscripts in the statistics of Chapter Two. Beyond that the fact that MSS gh(i) are higher and MSS Acx are lower is a further indication of the independence of MSS boc_2e_2 z ghi over against MSS Acx.

b. synoptic survey

Table 21

Additions Range of Variants

Adjectives	42	Names	95	Preposit's	150
Adverbs	31	Nouns	188	Pronouns	179
Articles	371	Numbers	12	Translit's	2
Conjunct's	174	Particles	33	Verbs	157
Interject's	4				

---

[74]At least they are not straight readings of the type manifest in MS A to the extent that it represents the fifth column of the Hexapla. Of course readings can and do come from other columns of the Hexapla (Aquila, Symmachus and Theodotion).

The one figure that stands out from all the rest is that for the article. It is higher than the combined totals for names and nouns. Both from the figure here and from the experience of entering and studying the data it is clear that this adding of the definite article is another of the Lucianic characteristics, although the difference between the Lucianic text and the majority text is one of degree not of kind.[75] In the Old Greek the use of the article was limited often in deference to and under the influence of Hebrew syntax and usage. As the Septuagint text came to be viewed from a Greek rather than a Hebrew perspective, one of the obvious anomalies was the inconsistent use of the article. Accordingly, as time passed the situation was addressed. That many of the additions were independent of the Lucianic manuscripts is clearly seen in the number of definite articles that are part of the majority text but not in the Old Greek. The variants under study here are independent of the majority, however, because the number of non-Lucianic manuscripts admitted is sufficiently low to exclude majority readings from consideration.

1. single word readings

The single word readings consist of a vast array of words that have been 'added' to the text as viewed from the perspective of both the Old Greek and the majority non-Lucianic text. Their use can be summarized as explanatory or explicative, and editorial.

Within the first category are such items as the definite articles, the nouns–both proper and common–and the pronouns. As noted, the largest category is the addition of the definite articles. That careful attention was given to the use of the article in the redaction of the Lucianic text can be seen not only from the number of additions here, but also from the number of omissions noted in that category.

It is possible to classify the patterns of addition of the article: with nouns that are accompanied by a personal pronoun or another noun in

---

[75]Brock observes that "While the tendency to add the article was very general, nevertheless it is in *L*[ucian] that this reaches its fullest extent" ("Recensions," p. 250).

the genitive case;[76] with nouns that are definite by context but did not have the article in the Old Greek (sometimes because the Hebrew *Vorlage* lacked the article, especially with nouns in the construct state); to provide a case marker for indeclinable proper nouns or transliterations; articular infinitives; and relative pronouns.

However, while they are able so to be described, and while they are extensive, these additions do not cover every such potential case. Thus where definite articles are added their use can be described–after all these are typical uses of the article–but it is not possible to predict where they will occur, or explain why other similar cases are not included.

The addition of names, nouns and pronouns to the text to make explicit what is either implicit or not clear is another of the characteristics of the Lucianic text. Brock concluded that "this text was designed for public reading (in whatever context, not necessarily just a lectionary one) ..." as evidenced by these additions that make "the text absolutely–one might sometimes say, painfully–clear to listeners ...."[77]

Beyond all of this the editorial work that has also served to make the Lucianic text distinctive is still evident. Two example illustrate this:

2:26
    Maj: και το παιδαριον Σαμουηλ επορευετο και εμεγαλυνετο
    Luc: και το παιδαριον Σαμουηλ επορευετο και εμεγαλυνετο

    Maj: και   αγαθον και μετα κυριου και μετα ανθρωπων
    Luc: και ην αγαθον   μετα κυριου και   ανθρωπων

3:12
    Maj: εν τη ημερα εκεινη επεγερω επι Ηλι παντα οσα
    Luc: εν τη ημερα εκεινη επεγερω επι Ηλι παντα οσα

---

[76]Martin lists "the use of genitive personal pronouns dependent on an anarthrous substantive" as a mark of translation Greek ("Criticism," p. 66). The addition of the article in these cases makes the text less like a translation.

[77]"Recensions," pp. 261-262.

Maj: ελαλησα   εις τον οικον αυτου αρξομαι και επετελεσω
Luc: ελαλησα και επι τον οικον αυτου αρξομαι και συντελεσω

Maj: "In that day I will raise up against Eli all things that I have said(;) against his
   house(;) I will begin and I will make an end."
Luc: "In that day I will raise up against Eli all things that I have said; and upon his
   house I will begin and I will complete it."

The majority text is ambiguous as regards punctuation (as indicated by
the semicolons enclosed in brackets), while the Lucianic text is not.

   2. *multiple word readings*

Table 22

Additions Multiple Word Readings

no. in group	total
2	141
3	52
4	25
5	7
6	3
7	4
8	5
8+	9

As can be seen the bulk of them are double readings as was the case
with transpositions. A question that arose in connection with these
additions was whether or not they are shared with the MT. The results
of the analysis are as follows:[78]

not in MT	157
in MT	71

Thus some two-thirds of these additions are not in the MT.

---

[78]To be included the readings had not only to share the MT reading, but in addition
to share the reading at the same point in the text.
   In addition to these 228 readings there were also 18 doublets.

By the time of Origen and the Hexapla the Hebrew text that was the forerunner of what is usually termed 'the MT' was in the ascendancy. It could easily be assumed from this that the additions relative to the Old Greek would be hexaplaric readings that bear a close relationship to the MT, inasmuch as the readings that Origen added in his fifth column, marked with the asterisk, reflected those in his Hebrew text that were lacking in his Greek text.[79] In fact, as these statistics show, this is not the case. Certainly there are 71 readings that are shared in common between the Lucianic text and the MT, but this is less than one-third of the total, with over 170 that are not traceable to the MT. It is the presence of such readings, noted also in other categories, that keep alive the intriguing question of the Hebrew *Vorlage* and the Greek archetype of the Lucianic text and the relationship they bear to the MT and the Old Greek.

Within this large body of variant readings there are numerous examples of the types of readings noted above. In chapter five alone there are five explanatory readings not found in the MT:

5:4 οι Αζωτιοι
5:6 τους Αζωτιους
5:8 οι Αζωτιοι
5:8 οι Αζωτιοι
5:10 οι Γεθθαιους

These all supply the subject or the object to make the sentence explicit.

The presence of doublets is one of the features of the Lucianic text. Perhaps the most fascinating one is found in 14:40. It presents two essentially identical texts except for one significant difference: two variant readings of the same Hebrew word. First in the example below is the reading of the majority text–including the Lucianic manuscripts–while the second reading is the later Lucianic doublet.

---

[79] The readings in the Greek but not in the Hebrew were naturally those already in his text which he marked with the obelus.

1. και ειπεν   παντι ανδρι Ισραηλ Υμεις εσεσθε
2. και ειπεν Σαουλ προς τον λαον Υμεις εσεσθε

1. εις δουλειαν και εγω και Ιωναθαν ο υιος μου εσομεθα
2. εις εν μερος και εγω και Ιωναθαν   εσομεθα

1. εις δουλειαν.
2. εις εν μερος.

The first time the translation reflects the letter variant עבד and the second time it represents the MT עבר. It is intriguing that both these readings should have found their way into one Greek text.

The final example preserves an anachronistic editorial comment:

18:3

    Maj: και διεθωτο Ιωναθαν και Δαυιδ   διαθηκην (> A)
    Luc: και διεθετο Ιωναθαν και Δαυιδ ο βασιλευς διαθηκην

David is called king as early as the return from the killing of Goliath.

Conclusions

The study in this chapter has looked at the Lucianic manuscripts to see what it is that sets them apart as a family. Two primary conclusions emerge: first, that the five Lucianic manuscripts witness to an archetype that was redacted; but second, that redaction, in the form that it exists today, is not complete, and/or has been reharmonized towards the majority text.

Evidence of the redaction can be seen in the characteristics that have been isolated in the analysis. They are summarized below in the order in which they were introduced:

    a. Σηλω for Old Greek Σηλωμ
    b. νουμηνια for νεομηνια
    c. αλως corrected to fem.
    d. ελεως corrected to 2nd decl. masc.
    e. most 1st aor. forms of ειπα corrected to 2nd aor.
    f. aor. pass. of γινομαι altered to aor. middle
    g. Ακχους for Old Greek Αγχους
    h. αρεστον for αγαθον in formula το αρεστον ενωπιον/εν οφθαλμοις

i. εχθες και τριτης for εχθες και τριτην
j. μαχαιρα for ρομφαια
k. προεφητευσεν for επροφητευσεν
l. Σεκελαγ for Σεκελακ

Evidence on the other hand that the redaction is only partial in the preserved witnesses can be seen from the following:

a. the partial substitutions of οτι with διοτι
b. the general use of πεδιον but the retention of some forms of αγρος
c. the substitution of some *koine* forms by their Attic equivalents
d. the addition of *koine* forms such as πλην to the text
e. the introduction of some better Greek syntax, but also the introduction of some Semitic style syntax, along with the retention of the overall Semitic style.
f. the retention of some of the forms altered in points e, f, h, and j above under 'characteristics'

Further evidence of the partial nature of the redaction as it exists today can also be seen in the trends that were isolated:

a. εν with the dative replaced by the simple dative
b. the frequent inclusion of the article
c. σημερον not used with ημερα
d. the addition of πας

The result is a text that on the one hand shares most readings in common with the manuscripts at large, but that on the other hand also has recensional readings that set the family apart.

CHAPTER IV

Analysis of the Lucianic Minority Variants

There are three general types of minority variants among the Lucianic manuscripts. The first type is unintentional errors such as haplography and dittography which arise whenever manuscripts are copied. They are recognized by comparing the variant reading with the Lucianic majority text. Such readings are well represented in the minority variants under study.

The second type is scribal emendation which arises during the copying process. In general terms minority variants that are not identifiable as errors, and that are not supported by non-Lucianic manuscripts, are regarded as scribal emendations in this study. They are most easily recognized when they have a discernible pattern, but in the case of the minority readings under study there are only three new characteristics among the hundreds of variants.

The third type of minority variant is harmonization. Manuscripts were not copied in isolation and over the centuries there was a tendency for manuscripts–especially distinctive manuscripts like the Lucianic manuscripts–to be harmonized with, or levelled to the better-known textual tradition. It was a frequent practice for scribes to make notes between lines and/or in the margins as well as to record readings from other manuscripts[1] and then these would at times find their way into the

---

[1] The third apparatus in B-M consists of readings from the later Greek traditions such as Aquila and Symmachus taken principally from notes in the manuscripts included in the second apparatus.

text. In addition to these more deliberate measures other variants found their way directly into the text when scribes consciously or unconsciously harmonized as they copied, often by the addition or omission of a letter or two. Because these readings are harmonizations to the larger tradition one of the keys to their recognition is their non-Lucianic manuscript support. Thus it is that in this study scribal emendation has generally been distinguished from harmonization on the basis of non-Lucianic manuscript support.

The minority variants in the five database categories fall into two divisions: that between omissions and additions on the one hand; and base text, substitutions and transpositions on the other. The latter do not alter the length of the text, while the former do. Most of the omission variants under consideration here are unintentional due to haplography. In the case of the addition variants it is more difficult because there are two basically similar types of variants: dittography and doublets. To distinguish between them, those minority readings that are synonymous with readings in the Lucianic text are counted as doublets, while those minority readings that are (essentially) identical with the Lucianic text are regarded as dittography. Thus the essence of 'doublet' is defined as 'synonymous' rather than 'identical.'

Statistics tables are again provided for these categories, although they have been slightly modified to accommodate the different circumstances here.[2] For the majority statistics it was sufficient to indicate if one of the two b manuscripts (b′ or *b*) shared a reading so that only the composite figure was used. Here, however, there are sufficient independent variants in each manuscript to warrant distinguishing between the two of them, so in the second table (manuscript families) they are listed separately.

---

[2] In the case of the majority variants it took at least three manuscripts to produce one (majority) reading. The essence was unity. For the minority variants each of the manuscripts is basically independent of the rest, despite the majority text they share in common. The essence is diversity.

In these minority variant categories the figures for the non-Lucianic manuscripts do not carry the importance and weight that they did for the majority text. There the witness was to the (one) Lucianic text. Here each of the Lucianic manuscripts is essentially separate (although there are some readings supported by two manuscripts) but the lists of the non-Lucianic manuscripts are combined. From this it is known which other manuscripts share readings, but not which readings.

1. Base text

This is the first of the categories that looks at the Lucianic majority text through the minority readings, however the context is also the readings accepted by Rahlfs for inclusion in his text. It would seem at first glance that these minority readings which are so far removed from both their archetype and from the Old Greek would not be any help in reconstructing the Old Greek. Some of the readings are letter variants to the Lucianic (majority) text, but some cannot be accounted for in this way and seem to be best accounted for as harmonizations. Despite the fact that they may have entered the text in this way and are not Lucianic in the same sense as the Lucianic majority text, in the overall history of the text they deserve to be considered on their own merits, not prejudged on the basis of their origin.

a. statistical analysis

Table 23

Lucianic Base Text Minority Readings

b	5	o	7	c_2	3
bo	2	oc_2	2	e_2	3
b c_2	1	o e_2	1	$c_2 e_2$	1
b e_2	0				

Total: 25

Table 24

Non-Lucianic Support for Minority Base Text Readings

b′	6	B	19	d	0	e	3	M	0
b	6	y	8	l	1	f	3	N	7
o	12	a₂	8	p	0	m	2	a	1
c₂	7			q	2	s	1	g	1
e₂	5			t	1	w	3	h	3
				z	1			i	3
								j	2
		A	9					n	2
		c	4					v	2
		x	6					b₂	2

Though the statistics are based on only a small sampling, it is interesting to note that readings read by only one Lucianic manuscript predominate over those shared by two. To the extent that this holds true it indicates independence among the individual manuscripts. Ms o has the largest number of readings–and also the highest number that are difficult to classify.

The figure for MS B is (comparatively) high because the Rahlfs text is based on MS B. For the rest of the categories it is not anticipated that MS B will play a significant role if it plays a part at all.

b. synoptic survey

Table 25

Base Text Range of Variants

Adjectives	0	Names	5	Preposit's	2
Adverbs	1	Nouns	4	Pronouns	1
Articles	1	Numbers	0	Translit's	1
Conjunct's	1	Particles	0	Verbs	9
Interject's	0				

The three parts of speech most in evidence are verbs, names and nouns. All of the verbs and names are letter variants of the (Lucianic) majority text while editorial change seems in evidence with some of the nouns.

1. single word readings

In 1:1 MSS c$_2$ Ba$_2$ share the name Ηλιου. The non-Lucianic majority reading is Ηλι which is shared by MS b,[3] MS o omits this and the surrounding words due to haplography, and MS e$_2$ has Ειλι(/Ιλι)[4]. At first it seems that MS c$_2$ has somehow preserved the Old Greek reading. Thus it is important to note that MS A has the letter variant form Ελιου. This manuscript is notorious for its irregular orthography and here it is significant that it alone of all the other manuscripts has a reading similar to MSS c$_2$ Ba$_2$. But of all the Lucianic manuscripts it is MS c$_2$ that has been most influenced by the hexaplaric text, and this is the most likely source of the reading in MS c$_2$ rather than any direct contact with or preservation of the Old Greek.

The second reading (1:11) ελωαι oc$_2$ A Nib$_2$ does not at first seem to be a clear Lucianic majority reading. Most of the non-Lucianic manuscripts read ελωε which is also shared by MS e$_2$, while MS b reads Ελωι. It appears as though the reading of MSS oc$_2$ was the Lucianic reading, as testified to by the letter variant of MS b. In the case of MS e$_2$ -αι- can easily become -ε-,[5] although in this case it may be a harmonization to the majority (non-Lucianic) reading.

At 6:18 the Lucianic manuscripts divide equally between two readings: σατραπων oc$_2$ Bya$_2$/σατραπιων be$_2$ rell. In the four occurrences of the words, the first two times the majority non-Lucianic text reads σατραπιων (both in chapter six), and the second two times it

---

[3]This is clearly influenced by the name 'Eli.'

[4]The former is the form shown in B-M, the latter is the standardized form used in the majority text.

[5]There are two other examples of this ε/αι interchange in this category: 14:33 Γεθθεμ/Γεθθαιμ/Γεθεμ, and 23:24 Ιεσσαιμουν/Ιεσσεμουν.

reads σατραπων.[6] Apart from the above reading in 6:18, the Lucianic
majority text reads σατραπων, although MS b has σατραπιων at 6:4,
and is joined by MS e$_2$ at 6:18. Thus the key to the absence of a majority
Lucianic reading at 6:18 is to be found in MS e$_2$ which has been har-
monized to the majority reading, fluctuating as it does between the two
forms of the noun.

There are five words in this category that are not letter variants
and are best accounted for as harmonizations:

> 1:11 ανδρων c$_2$e$_2$ B A/ανδρος bo maj.
> 2:25 υπερ *b*oc$_2$⁚ B e h/περι *b*'c$_2$*e$_2$ maj.
> 6:15 θυσιας *b* Bya$_2$ Nn*/θυσιαν maj.
> 10 24 αυτω ομοιος o B fsw/ομοιος αυτω boc$_2$e$_2$ maj.
> 28:22 πορευση e$_2$ B/πορευη boc$_2$e$_2$ maj.

Of these the most difficult to account for is the reading in 10:24.
From the perspective of the Old Greek the majority of the manuscripts
(including MSS bc$_2$e$_2$) have the transposition, leaving MSS o B fsw in the
untransposed position. Conversely, from the perspective of the Lucianic
majority, MS o has transposed the Lucianic order, an order that moves
towards Semitic rather than Greek syntax, but which also moves towards
the Old Greek text.

2. multiple word readings

No Lucianic minority readings are base text multiple word
variants.

2. Omissions

In this and the remaining categories the focus is no longer on the
Old Greek text although some of the readings are supported by MS B.
Instead it is possible to concentrate on the Lucianic text as seen through
a representative group of the Lucianic variants.

---

[6]The Rahlfs text reads σατραπων with MS B all four times.

Of all the categories Omissions has been the most difficult to assess because widely divergent influences can appear to converge as manuscripts and families omit (or appear to omit) for entirely different reasons. In the case of these minority readings the situation is more focused. A large number of the variants were omitted from the Lucianic manuscripts by scribal error in copying. For the first time the readings that remain after excluding the unintentional errors are actual omissions of a text–the Lucian text–rather than witnesses to a shorter text.

a. statistical analysis

To provide a meaningful point of comparison the statistics are confined to the omission readings that remain after all the readings that can be accounted for as due to haplography have been removed.[7]

Table 26

Lucianic Minority Omissions of the Base Text

b	69	o	62	c_2	18
bo	4	oc_2	1	e_2	35
$b\,c_2$	1	$o\ e_2$	1	c_2e_2	1
$b\ e_2$	5				

Total: 197

---

[7]430 words were excluded from the count for this reason. To qualify for inclusion as such it was necessary to be able to identify in the Lucianic majority text the two identical words/endings/etc. of which the copyist only read one as his eye skipped to the second.

Table 27

Non-Lucianic Support for Lucianic Minority Omissions

b′	77	B	4	d	33	e	4	M	1
b	38	y	10	l	5	f	4	N	4
o	68	a_2	11	p	7	m	1	a	5
c_2	21			q	5	s	2	g	10
e_2	42			t	5	w	1	h	4
				z	5			i	7
								j	0
		A	3					n	5
		c	32					v	11
		x	29					b_2	0

Of first importance are the individual statistics for MS b′ and MS
o. They are significantly higher than the rest, especially MS *b* and MS c_2,
and are principally due to scribal error apart from haplography.[8]
Second, it is important to note how few of the readings are shared by any
two of the Lucianic manuscripts. These statistics for the double manu-
script support illustrate the fact that the minor omissions are basically
confined to individual manuscripts with no discernible trends so far.

In the statistics for the majority omissions MS d among the non-
Lucianic manuscripts appeared the closest to the Lucianic manuscripts,
but it was noted there the degree to which this manuscript abbreviates,
a fact that is not related to the omissions of the Lucianic manuscripts.
Similarly the number of omissions shared here with MSS cx cannot, on the
basis of this category alone, be assumed to be of any significance. While
MSS ghiz showed affinity with the Lucianic majority text, no such affinity
is in evidence with the minority readings so far.

b. synoptic survey
     As was the case for the statistical table above, this survey does not
include readings excluded due to haplography.

---

[8]Even when the readings caused by haplography are excluded, readings still remain
that can only be explained in their context as scribal error.

Table 28

Omissions Range of Variants

Adjectives	8	Names	9	Preposit's	22
Adverbs	5	Nouns	37	Pronouns	35
Articles	48	Numbers	1	Translit's	0
Conjunct's	19	Particles	6	Verbs	7
Interject's	0				

The most frequent omissions are of the article, which type of omission was also a factor with the majority text. Also prominent are the omission of nouns, pronouns and prepositions, although as will be seen no patterns have emerged.

1. single word readings

As is seen for the statistics under multiple word readings, the majority of the omissions are due to scribal error apart from haplography. Among those that are not due to error are some interesting examples. One such example from MS c_2 is found in 1:8:

Maj: και ειπεν αυτη Ελκανα ο ανηρ αυτης Αννα.
c_2: και ειπεν αυτη Ελκανα ο ανηρ αυτης Αννα.

Maj: και ειπεν αυτω ιδου εγω κυριε. και ειπεν αυτη τι εστιν
c_2: και ειπεν   ιδου εγω   και ειπεν   τι

Maj: σοι οτι κλαιεις;
c_2:   οτι κλαιεις;

Twice c_2 omits the pronoun after και ειπεν. The first time the shorter text is shared with MSS Acx dpqtz efmsw Mghnvwb$_2$,[9] and the second time with MS d which may be coincidental. The omission of κυριε is shared with MSS y Acx dpqt, and appears thereby to be a hexaplaric omission. It is possible that there are two types of harmonization here: one internal, one external. 1:8 begins with και ειπεν αυτη which is

---

[9] Only MSS Bya$_2$ boe$_2$ N have the (longer) reading.

read by all the database manuscripts, and when the phrase reoccurs the first time (και ειπεν ...), the majority of manuscripts (Acx dpqtz efmsw Maghnvb$_2$) omit αυτω as pleonastic, as does MS c$_2$ which harmonizes with the majority (the external harmonization), but MS c$_2$ goes one step further by harmonizing the whole passage with the omission of the pronouns (αυτω, αυτη) after και ειπεν both times (the internal harmonization).

Some examples of haplography are 6:9 ει εις > εις b′ y*a$_2$ dp Nh; 8:19 βασιλευς εσται > βασιλευσεται bn*; 9:9 εμπροσθεν εν > εμπροσθεν e$_2$ Ac e Na$^{a?}$n*v <44>; and 23:22 ταχει εκει > εκει (homoioteleuton).

2. *multiple word readings*

Most of the readings in the minority omissions category are multiple word variants.

Table 29

Omissions Multiple Word Readings

no. in group	total
2	42
3	18
4	14
5	9
6	2
7	3
8	1
9	2
10	1
11	1
11+	5

The variants were also grouped according to the following classifications:

accidental omissions
haplog.	57	
homoio.	6	
error	6	
total:	69	70.4%

intentional omissions
editorial	25	
not clear	4	
total:	29	29.6%

In the first category, though homoioteleuton is a subset of haplography, it is listed separately for the six places where it was a factor.[10] A variant is listed as an 'error' when it is not recognizable as an intentional omission, but the passage does not make sense in the absence of the reading. An example is found in 20:11 where the omission of προς Δαυιδ πορευου και μενε εις αγρον results in an anacoluthon. 70% of the multiple word omissions are unintentional errors.

The order of the listing of the two categories 'accidental' and 'intentional' is intended. As the number of readings studied increased it became evident that most of them were unintentional omissions. Thus only when efforts to classify the readings as unintentional omissions were unsuccessful were they considered intentional omissions. 'Editorial changes' are readings that alter the meaning of the passage in a meaningful way. For instance at 16:15 the omission of κυριου πορευθεντων removes the Lord as the source of the evil spirit that tormented Saul. Approximately 30% of multiple word omissions were deemed to be intentional alterations.

There are two important observations in connection with the omissions. First, it is only possible to classify these readings by reference to the Lucianic text. For convenience in the research the entire database was printed out in hard copy. As each of these variants was researched it was necessary to reconstruct the Lucianic text among the omissions,

---

[10]Thus there are 63 readings overall for haplography.

transpositions, etc. before the beginning and the end of the haplography could be recognized. In no instance was an unclassified Lucianic minority omission able to be recognized as a meaningful variant in any non-Lucianic text.

Second, these variants stand as a warning. At 5:10 MSS b y Ac z e gv omit eight words. Although MS b is among good company, the omission is due to haplography (ασκαλωνα–ασκαλωνα), and it is one of many such examples. Thus it is probable that the agreement of MS b with the other manuscripts is coincidental.

An instructive omission passage is found at 25:6. To understand the picture clearly it is necessary to refer to the Old Greek, the Lucianic majority text, and the reading of MS e$_2$ which is the reading under study:

OG: και συ υγιαινων και ο οικος σου και παντα τα σα
boc$_2$: και συ υγιαινων και   παντα τα σα (> o)
e$_2$: και συ

OG: υγιαινοντα
boc$_2$: υγιαινοντα και ο οικος σου
e$_2$: υγιαινοντα

For the most part the example is straightforward as regards the Lucianic majority transposition. In turn the text of MS e$_2$ appears at first like haplography, except that the scribe would have to have written και συ expecting to pick up υγιαινων but picked up υγιαιοντα instead, and written it. What is troubling is that the example only seems explicable with reference to the Old Greek, because if it were based on the Lucianic text the haplography would leave the now later και ο οικος σου unaccounted for. Readings such as this one indicate that there is a complexity lurking behind these manuscripts for which the characteristics and patterns are but the preamble.

3. Substitutions

This category studies the places where individual (or less frequently, combinations of two[11]) Lucianic manuscripts have readings variant to the Lucianic (majority) text.

a. statistical analysis

Table 30

Minority Lucianic Substitutions

b	338	o	229	c_2	85
bo	29	oc_2	18	e_2	192
b c_2	13	o e_2	15	c_2e_2	17
b e_2	26				

Total: 962

Table 31

Non-Lucianic Support for Minority Substitutions

b'	354	B	7	d	26	e	22	M	3
b	223	y	20	l	2	f	30	N	23
o	291	a_2	53	p	30	m	24	a	44
c_2	133			q	10	s	21	g	72
e_2	250			t	13	w	12	h	28
				z	19			i	28
								j	4
		A	25					n	18
		c	93					v	56
		x	71					b_2	6

It is significant that MS b' and MS o again have the most variants. Such patterns were not able to emerge in the base text statistics due to insufficient readings, but for the omissions category these two manuscripts far exceeded the other three. While the separation between the two groups–MS b' and MS o; and MS b, MS c_2 and MS e_2–is not as wide

---

[11]By definition there are no readings here supported by more than two manuscripts.

here, MS b´ and MS o do lead the others both in single readings and to a much lesser extent, in double readings.[12]

Among the non-Lucianic manuscripts the figures for MSS cx g appear to warrant mention because they are significantly higher than the rest. In fact this is not the case, as can be seen from a comparison with the corresponding majority substitutions table. For that table there were 1303 readings under consideration, with the Lucianic manuscripts each sharing between 1225 and 1284 of the total readings. For this table there are 962 readings under consideration. Of this total, 118 are shared by two Lucianic manuscripts, the remaining 844 being single readings, and the highest number of readings shared by any one of them is 354 (MS b´).

From these comparatively low statistics it can be seen that many more single readings are under consideration in this category than was the case with the majority readings, and correspondingly percentages for the non-Lucianic manuscripts drop well below the level of affinity. Thus the Lucianic minority readings do not indicate further recensional affinities either among themselves or outside of the family.

b. synoptic survey

As was the case for the majority readings, the format of the table for the types of substitution variants is different from the others. Because there is a direct point of contact–these substitutions relate directly to the Lucianic text–it is possible to indicate whether the reading is a variant form of the same word, a synonym of that word, or a different word.

In addition, another category has been added within the table: letter variants. It was noted in the majority text analysis that few letter variants are present in the majority text, but that is not the case here, as can be seen from the total of 289 readings. The addition of the letter

---

[12]It was noted in the Introduction (pp. 10-11) that in the last two books of Reigns MSS bc₂ and oe₂ often read together. The small amount of shared minority readings in evidence here bears no relationship to the patterns there.

variants category means that there are two categories–letter variants and inner Greek–that can overlap, so it is helpful to consider the role of each.

The letter variant category is reserved for unintentional errors that arose because of confusion over letters that were pronounced alike such as: ι/η/υ/ει, οι/υι, ο/ω, αι/ε, δ/θ.[13] The 'inner Greek' category is reserved for readings which, though similar to the letter variants, are deemed to have been intentional. One of the major sources for such readings is the frequent switch between singular and plural or vice versa, where the change often involves a difference of only one or two letters, such as ειπεν and ειπον, αυτου and αυτων, or even ειπεν and ειδεν. While the change is only small, these are not letters that were usually confused, so they have been counted separately.

Although the presence of the two categories was found to be useful, there were the inevitable readings that were difficult to decide, especially with singular and plural forms of the same word, as to whether the alterations were intentional or not. Each variant had to be weighed on its own merits, because even with the same manuscript there are contradictory trends present, or perhaps more accurately, there may not be any actual trends.[14]

---

[13]This includes what is often termed itacisms (or more accurately iotacisms), but is not confined to them.

[14]There is always a danger of seeking system and order where none may exist. Many of the minority variants are the result of the copying process that involved an unknown number of scribes with conceivably different, and even at times opposite, impacts on the textual tradition.

Table 32

Substitutions Range of Variants

Adjectives	12	Names	171	Preposit's	26
Same	6	Same	0	Same	0
Synon.	2	Synon.	135	Synon.	9
Diff.	4	Diff.	36	Diff.	17
Adverbs	5	Nouns	71	Pronouns	84
Same	0	Same	28	Same	59
Synon.	0	Synon.	34	Synon.	19
Diff.	5	Diff.	9	Diff.	6
Articles	32	Numbers	2	Translit's	0
Same	30	Same	1	Same	0
Synon.	1	Synon.	0	Synon.	0
Diff.	1	Diff.	1	Diff.	0
Conjunct's	3	Particip's	10	Verbs	87
Same	0	Same	9	Same	43
Synon.	2	Synon.	1	Synon.	38
Diff.	1	Diff.	0	Diff.	6
Interject's	0	Particles	6	Inner-Gr.	164
Same	0	Same	0		
Synon.	0	Synon.	4	Let-var's	289
Diff.	0	Diff.	2		

The three categories that stand out are letter variants, inner Greek variants, and names. Of the letter variants some 172 are verbs. These are frequent because the vowels readily invite confusion, especially the η/ει interchange, since both represent legitimate forms.

In a text of this nature which has non-Greek names it is to be expected that they will suffer poorly in the copying process. The division of the text between majority and minority readings left these variant, and even aberrant, forms of the names for this section.[15]

---

[15]Many of the forms could also be listed as letter variants, but because they have their own category they are listed here.

In addition to the 172 verbs in the letter variants category, another 87 are in the verb category. Verbs were included in their own category when they were synonyms, and also when the difference between the minority verb and the majority reading was more substantive than just a letter variant or an inner Greek alteration.

1. single word readings

Among the plethora of mainly unrelated and uncoordinated readings three characteristics emerge. First, in the majority (Lucianic and non-Lucianic) text, the word χριστος occurs 12 times.[16] In all but two of these[17] MS e₂ reads χρηστος instead.

The second characteristic is related to one noted for the majority text where the augment in the word προφητευω was seen always to be placed between the prefix and the verb. Going one step further, MS b′ reads with a double augment as in: επροεφητευσαν.[18]

The third characteristic is the preference in MS b′ for the form νωτον over the Lucianic majority νοτον.[19]

Beyond these another reading is of interest. At 2:20 all of the Lucianic manuscripts have variant readings:

bo: ανταποδωσει
c₂: ανταποδωσει σοι
e₂: ανταποδω   σοι

---

[16]2:10, 2:35, 12:3, 12:5, 16:6, 24:7 (*bis*), 24:11, 26:9, 26:11, 26:16, 26:23.

[17]2:35, 24:7. In the second instance where MS e₂ does not substitute, B-M thought that they detected the latter reading in the first hand of MS c₂—that is to say they indicated it as "c₂*(vid)".
    For 24:7 H-P have χρηστω as the reading for MS 93 (e₂), and do not list any variant to the majority reading χριστω for MS 127 (c₂), which may indicate a slip in B-M of 'c₂*' for 'e₂*'.

[18]19:20, 19:21 (*bis*), 19:24.

[19]14:5, 27:10, 30:1, 30:14 (*bis*), and 30:27.

It would appear that only MS c₂ has retained the full reading, the omission of σοι in MSS bo, and the omission of -σει in MS e₂ being due to haplography.

Although there are many variants that have been created unintentionally it does not mean that all of them have been so created. One such example is at 15:26 where MS o reads the verb βασιλευειν for the majority ειναι βασιλεα.

2. multiple word readings

Of the 962 total words in this section only 95 are part of multiple readings, and the rest are single word readings. There are 41 double readings, three triple and one quadruple, and of these 24 are letter variants. There are no further characteristics among these readings.

At 2:14 the reading εν τη λουτηρι is shared with, and is possibly from, Aquila. It is instructive to compare the reading at 4:6 with the hexaplaric manuscripts:

```
OG: η κραυγη                        η μεγαλη αυτη (= maj)
oe₂: η φωνη                         η μεγαλη αυτη
Hex: η κραυγη του αλαλαγμου         η μεγαλη αυτη Acx dpqtz
  c₂: η φωνη του αλαλαγμου          η μεγαλη αυτη (sub ※)
  b: η φωνη του αλαλαγματος του μεγαλου
```

It is difficult to determine the sequence in these split readings. The only guide is the overall knowledge of the characteristics of the text. It was seen in chapter two that the Lucianic manuscripts contain much hexaplaric material, but such a synchronic study does not answer diachronic questions that a group of variants like this poses as to when in the history of the text particular readings became part of the tradition. All the Lucianic manuscripts share η φωνη, and MSS boc₂ have η μεγαλη αυτη as well.

It seems probable that the hexaplaric material which the reading of MS b developed,[20] was added to MSS bc$_2$ independent of the original Lucianic recension.[21]

At 18:1 there is an example of deliberate editing. The majority (Lucianic and non-Lucianic) text reads: "and his soul was knit to the soul of David" whereas MS b′ reads "and the soul of David was knit to his soul," the reverse order.

Among the multiple readings a good example of an inner Greek variant is found in 30:22:

OG, bc$_2$e$_2$: ου κατεδιωξαν
 o: ουκ απεδιωξαν

By the simple, and perhaps unconscious, τ/π interchange the text retained its basic meaning.

4. Transpositions
 a. statistical analysis

Table 33

Minority Transpositions of the Lucianic Text

b	36	o	25	c$_2$	10
bo	4	oc$_2$	0	e$_2$	20
b c$_2$	3	o e$_2$	0	c$_2$e$_2$	2
b e$_2$	0				

Total: 100

---

[20]This example serves to illustrate the independence of MS b that resulted in such a high number of substitution readings for this category.

[21]This approach is preferred over the idea of the hexaplaric reading having been omitted by the other two manuscripts.

Table 34

Non-Lucianic Support for Minority Transpositions

b′	39	B	0	d	1	e	2	M	0
b	24	y	1	l	1	f	1	N	4
o	29	a₂	1	p	2	m	1	a	0
c₂	15			q	2	s	1	g	0
e₂	22			t	2	w	1	h	3
				z	4			i	0
								j	0
		A	2					n	3
		c	0					v	0
		x	1					b₂	0

It is manuscript b′ that again stands out as the most independent of the Lucianic tradition, while MS c₂ is the closest to the tradition. Confirmation that these are sub-Lucianic readings lies readily at hand in the figures for the non-Lucianic manuscripts which are all so low.

b. synoptic survey

As was the case with the majority transposition readings, no chart of the parts of speech is included here because the entry in the database does not tag all the elements of the transposition, and those that are tagged are selected for layout convenience in the database rather than to portray relationships. As a consequence it is not possible to compile meaningful statistics of the type included with the other categories.

1. single word readings

From the perspective of the Lucianic text some of these readings are substitutions, and as such suffer from the same type of errors already noted, especially letter variants. Those readings that remain after excluding these substitutions are examples of minority transpositions of the Lucianic text.

The first example in 1:1 is well known as one of the remedies for the abrupt beginning of the MT text. The Lucianic text shares part of the hexaplaric remedy (και εγενετο ανθρωπος) and reads και ανθρωπος ην. Ms b΄, ever the adventuresome one, has και ην ανθρωπος which better reflects Hebrew order, whether or not the scribe was aware of this.

When a scribe alters the order of a text that bears quite heavily the impact of its origins as a translation from a Semitic language into an Indo-European language it is to be expected that the changes will be more in line with the syntax of the target language than the source language. Although this is certainly in evidence here it does not account for all of the variants.

Some examples of moving towards a better style are found at 1:5, 2:25, and 13:11 where the subject precedes the verb; 10:9 subject, indirect object; 20:2 "big thing or little," not "a thing big or small;" 21:5 indirect object after verb; 11:2 "every right eye," not "every eye right."

However, other examples cannot be explained in that way: 10:24 verb, subject, indirect object; 24:11 subject last; 25:39 indirect object, direct object.

Finally two further examples are interesting. At 6:19 and 22:18 MS b΄ has an unusual sequence with the numbers:

6:19
    Luc: εβδομηκοντα ανδρας και πεντηκοντα χιλιαδας ανδρων
    b΄: εβδομηκοντα ανδρας και πεντηκοντα   ανδρων χιλιαδας

22:18
    Luc: πεντηκοντα ανδρας
    b΄:   ανδρας και πεντηκοντα

Second, in 28:14 Saul asks the medium at Endor to describe the form of the figure that she sees. The Old Greek records her as saying that she sees an ανδρα ορθιον, "an upright man;" whereas MSS be_2[22] read the letter variant ανδρα ορθριον, "a man early." Ορθριον is also found in MS b΄, but the(/a) scribe, recognizing that the word was an adverb and

---

[22]The reading is also in MSS y A m Ngh, and may have been the source of the reading for the Lucianic manuscripts.

not an adjective, moved it after the verb αναβαινων where it logically belongs once admitted to the text.

2. *multiple word readings*

For the most part the twenty-two readings in this category share the same characteristics as the single readings: some are letter variants, some move in the direction of Greek word order–but some appear to move in the opposite direction–while others have a different order for no apparent reason.

Perhaps the most significant is a series of 15 words which MS o transposed from 8:6 to 8:12.[23] The passage does not fit the new context, and was possibly originally omitted by mistake, later inserted between columns, and then subsequently copied to the wrong column.

It is clear then that among all the Lucianic manuscripts some minority readings alter the word order of the Lucianic text, but it is not done in any systematic or predictable way. There is no evidence of systematic recensional activity. Those readings that are not accidental are incidental in the overall history of the manuscripts.

5. *Additions*

Because the point of reference in the database for the division of the minority variants was not the Lucianic text, this category includes variants to additions that from the perspective of the Lucianic text are straight substitutions. As such they share many of the same characteristics that were noted above in that category. What remains are additions to the Lucianic text.

---

[23]That is to say the words are not where they belong at 8:6 at all, but are read at 8:12.

a. statistical analysis

Table 35

Lucianic Minority Additions

b	122	o	67	c_2	51
bo	10	oc_2	2	e_2	64
$b\,c_2$	7	$o\,e_2$	4	c_2e_2	8
$b\ e_2$	13				

Total: 348

Table 36

Non-Lucianic Support for Minority Additions

b′	138	B	0	d	8	e	4	M	1
b	90	y	0	l	4	f	4	N	4
o	83	a_2	9	p	12	m	3	a	4
c_2	68			q	8	s	1	g	15
e_2	89			t	7	w	4	h	12
				z	14			i	10
								j	2
		A	21					n	3
		c	20					v	3
		x	22					b_2	1

This time it is only MS b′ that stands out as having the most variants, while at the other end it is again MS c_2 that has the least number of readings. The fact that MSS Acx share more readings than all the rest of the non-Lucianic manuscripts, though only at a comparatively low figure, serves as a reminder that one of the prime sources of additions in the Lucianic manuscripts was hexaplaric readings. This finds further endorsement from the readings shared with MSS ghiz which were noted as reading with the Lucianic manuscripts, especially in chapters seventeen and eighteen.

b. synoptic survey

Table 37

Additions Range of Variants

Adjectives	8	Inner-Gr	76	Particles	11
Adverbs	13	Names	10	Preposit's	26
Articles	86	Nouns	29	Pronouns	35
Conjunct's	32	Numbers	3	Verbs	19

It is again the definite article that is prominent here as was the case with majority omissions and additions, and minority omissions. That their inclusion is not confined to their accompanying nouns can be seen from the low number of nouns added. Next in frequency are the inner Greek variants which serves to remind that these are minority readings.

1. single word readings

Many of these readings are Lucianic minority substitutions (as variants to additions) and are subject to the types of errors that have already been noted. Rather than repeat these, the study concentrates on some of the (Lucianic) additions.

At 1:3 MSS be₂ read εκεινος and MS o reads εκει. The former reading is shared with MS A, and in turn is the only representation/ translation of the MT ההוא. While harmonization could account for the introduction of the reading, the next example is more difficult.

At 10:13 MS b reads εις τον βουνον Βαμα for the Lucianic majority reading εις τον βουνον. The MT reads הבמה, and apart from the reading of MS b is not otherwise represented in the database manu-scripts. These are some of the examples of the Lucianic texts alone, or with a minority of manuscripts, containing or preserving[24] the reading of the MT.

It was noted that MS b′ has the highest number of readings in this category, and they are in evidence throughout. The result is best described as a fuller text, with some additions of the verb 'to be' to otherwise verbless clauses; the addition of the definite article, especially with proper nouns; the addition of personal pronouns to make explicit what was already implicit, to mention some of the more obvious examples.

2. multiple word readings

Table 38

Additions Multiple Word Readings

no. in group	total
2	18
3	5
4	7

Total: 31

Distribution of Multiple Word Readings

doublets	6
dittog.	6
hex.	6
editing	13

From these the hexaplaric readings are selected for analysis because this type of reading has not been noted in detail previously. All of the readings are from MS c$_2$. In 1:19 (και ηλθεν), and 1:26 (κε μου) the readings are marked with asterisks and are shared with MS A (and

---

[24]It is not possible from the perspective of this study to know whether the manuscripts 'contain' these readings from the original redaction (which may have Hebraized) or from harmonization, or whether they 'preserve' the readings as part of the witness to their Hebrew *Vorlage*.

MSS cx in 1:19). In 2:14 (εις τον λουτηρα) the reading is shared just with MS A. Field, on evidence independent of the Lucianic text, says that this reading is from Aquila.

At first glance it does not appear as though the next reading is hexaplaric (18:6 και εις απαντησιν Σαουλ) because it is supported only by MSS c₂ g. However MSS Acx dlpqtz j have the reading just a few words later in the text, or in other words it has been included in the Lucianic text in the same vicinity as the other manuscripts, though not at precisely the same point. Such readings included in the text at different places within the same vicinity often owe their origin to a marginal gloss.

In the course of the analysis of the Lucianic text in the context of the database manuscripts it was found that such readings–apparently unique readings of the Lucianic text shared by other manuscripts in the same general vicinity–are not infrequent.[25]

The final two examples are hexaplaric readings on the authority of manuscripts Acx: 22:11 (του κυ) and 29:9 (καθως αγγελος θυ).

All these readings bear the hallmarks of harmonization, some even betraying their origin as marginal glosses.

Conclusions

Only three minor characteristics emerge:

a. χρηστος for χριστος in MS e₂
b. double augment, επροεφητευσαν, in MS b′
c. νωτον for νοτον in MS b′.

---

[25]A total of 66 were isolated throughout the 31 chapters. A classic example is found in 2:31-32:

2:31 και ουκ εσται σου	πρεσβυτης εν		οικω μου Acx Thdt
2:32 και ουκ εσται	πρεσβυτης εν τω	οικω σου bc₂(sub ※)e₂ g
2:32 και ουκ εσται σου/σοι πρεσβυτης εν (τω) οικω μου bc₂ Acx g rell.

The second and third readings are at different places in v. 32.

It has not been possible to arrive at a theory comprehensive enough to account for all of the readings, first because of the ravages of the copying process in general, and harmonization to the better-known tradition in particular; but second, while it follows from the evidence that the archetype was more characteristic than the text as it exists today, it is not known just how consistent it was.

That the text is unified can be seen both from the majority and the minority statistics. In the majority statistics, readings supported by all the Lucianic manuscripts far outweigh those supported by only three. In the minority statistics there is a preponderance of readings supported by individual Lucianic manuscripts.

Since the minority readings are so diversified, it follows that once they have been discarded in those instances where there is a majority reading, or the reading that best represents the minority readings has been selected in the absence of a majority reading, what remains is the form of the text when the individual manuscripts diverged.

This picture would be clouded if the minority variants bore witness to any siginificant degree of independent recensional activity. As it is, there is no evidence of independent sensitivity to the Lucianic tradition on the part of any of the manuscripts, since none extends any of the characteristics isolated in Chapter Three.

Conclusion

The research in Chapter Two (especially when coupled with the data in the Appendix) has clearly indicated that the Lucianic manuscripts do not share the distinctive characteristics of MS B that set it apart as the exemplar of the Old Greek.

The acceptance of MS B as the exemplar of the Old Greek has served scholarship well, and is further supported by the results of this study. A definite relationship exists between MS B and MS A in the non-hexaplaric readings that accords with the claim that the text of MS B is the type of text that underlay the work of Origen in the preparation of his fifth column. Further, the statistics of other families such as MSS d(l)pqtz evidence the type of relationship between them and MS B (as well as between MS A) to be expected from a sub-hexaplaric family. Consequently there is no reason now to disturb this relationship so that the designation of the Lucianic manuscripts as Old Greek can be retained. Clearly they are not Old Greek in the sense that MS B and MS A (and their congeners) are Old Greek.

As noted, Cross has suggested that the proto-Lucianic text "was essentially [O]G with intruded Palestinian readings," while Barthélemy described it as "la Septante ancienne, plus ou moins abâtardie et corrompue." In the light of the evidence from this study such positions must be reconsidered and modified.

It is clear from the analysis in Chapter Three that discernible characteristics in the Lucianic text set it apart as a recension, but at the same time the text in its present form is only a partial redaction in that while some of the characteristics are consistent, others are not entirely so, while still other patterns are no more than trends.

This analysis was a necessary prelude to the creation of the Lucianic majority text found in Volume I. By adopting the method described there it has been possible to reconstruct the archetype of the extant Lucianic manuscripts. While methodologically there is no valid reason why family minority readings could not preserve archetype readings against the majority, in the case of the Lucianic manuscripts there is no evidence of this. The minority readings almost completely lack any systematic patterns, and where pattern is in evidence no sensitivity to the general recensional character of the majority text is to be seen.

If it could be established that the four manuscripts (counting the archetype of b′ and *b* as one manuscript) diverged soon after the fourth century redaction that Brock traced to Antioch in Syria, then it would follow from the analysis that the Lucianic majority text represents the work of the fourth century "Lucian."

However, before it can be concluded that this majority text is the same as the fourth century text, the nature of the majority text itself must be considered. As the text stands today it is a partial redaction with harmonization to non-Lucianic majority readings as a significant factor.

Thus these four manuscripts in their majority witness testify to their archetype as a somewhat later–there are no datable characteristics–copy of the original work which Brock unhesitatingly dated to the fourth century on the evidence of the Syrian Church Fathers.

It is necessary now for future research to take a fresh look at the relationships between the Lucianic (majority) text, the Hebrew texts, and the Old Latin, the principal sources of the conclusion that the Lucianic text is (essentially) the Old Greek. The analysis of these relationships must begin from the premise that the Lucianic text in 1 Reigns is not the Old Greek, and from there establish the nature of the interrelationships.

Appendix

The statistical analysis in Chapter Two was confined to three families of manuscripts: Bya_2, Acx and boc_2e_2. This Appendix contains the corresponding statistics for all of the manuscripts in the database, i.e. the degree of support among the manuscripts and families for the collation manuscript minority readings.

Because these statistics fell outside of the primary focus of the original analysis they were not included in Chapter Two, but because they provide opportunity for further study in manuscript relationships they are appended. Some observations to assist in interpreting them are included.

It is important to remember that the figures give only the total number of readings each manuscript has in common with the collation manuscript. It is not possible to ascertain from these figures how many readings are actually shared in common with any other manuscript(s). For 1 Reigns the manuscripts were grouped by families on the basis of the shared readings in B-M, not on the statistical analysis. There are thus two separate issues here: the frequency of readings shared with the collation manuscript, and the frequency of shared readings among the manuscripts. The former results in the statistical tables, the second, ascertained elsewhere, pre-determined the family groupings. The fact that the families consistently share readings is only confirmation of the original observations.

These statistics have been adjusted in the same manner as those included in Chapter Two, and as detailed there.[1] It would appear from the statistics that some manuscripts do not belong in their respective families because of the disparity of their numbers. The principal reason for this is that no adjustment has been made for physical lacunae. Those most seriously affected are MSS l M j,[2] and they have significantly lower figures in most categories when compared to the other members of their respective families.[3]   In the following tables the lines where these lacunae affect the statistics are placed within square brackets.

---

[1]See pp. 41-45.

[2]Where physical dammage is a factor, the information in the respective tables for the affected manuscript(s) is enclosed in square brackets.

[3]Not all of the tables are affected by these lacunae. For instance, of the eight manuscripts that have physical lacunae (A M g h j l m v), only that of MS M covers any of the hexaplaric material in chapters 17 and 18.

Ms B as the collation manuscript
  a. Base Text

Table 39

Mss	Total Minority Readings	Total as % of B
B	519	100.0
y	336	64.7
a₂	356	68.6
b′	58	11.2
b	58	11.2
o	65	12.5
c₂	62	12.0
e₂	58	11.2
A	234	45.1
c	178	34.3
x	196	37.8
d	91	17.5
[l	44	8.5]
p	97	18.7
q	102	19.7
t	100	19.3
z	94	18.1
e	145	27.9
f	128	24.7
m	115	22.2
s	125	24.1
w	137	26.4
[M	38	7.3]
N	120	23.1
a	110	21.2
[g	66	12.7]
h	103	19.9
i	127	24.5
[j	69	13.3]
n	171	33.0
v	82	15.8
b₂	123	23.7

Appendix

b. Omissions (MS B)

Table 40

Mss	Total Minority Readings	Total as % of B
B	118	100.0
y	70	59.3
a_2	62	52.5
b′	12	10.2
b	5	4.2
o	10	8.5
c_2	8	6.8
e_2	6	5.1
A	14	11.9
c	17	14.4
x	19	16.1
d	20	17.0
[l	5	4.2]
p	8	6.8
q	6	5.1
t	4	3.4
z	12	10.2
e	12	10.2
f	3	2.5
m	8	6.8
s	8	6.8
w	3	2.5
[M	2	1.7]
N	3	2.5
a	11	9.3
g	5	4.2
h	8	6.8
i	11	9.3
[j	0	]
n	6	5.1
v	20	17.0
b_2	7	5.9

c. Omissions–hexaplaric (MS B)

Table 41

Mss	Total Minority Readings	Total as % of B
B	800	100.0
y	800	100.0
a_2	353	44.1
b'	12	1.5
b	8	1.0
o	3	0.4
c_2	1	0.1
e_2	2	0.3
A	0	
c	104	13.0
x	98	12.3
d	40	5.0
l	1	0.1
p	0	
q	1	0.1
t	9	1.1
z	0	
e	14	1.8
f	109	13.6
m	108	13.5
s	107	13.4
w	11	1.4
[M	0	]
N	800	100.0
a	800	100.0
g	104	13.0
h	87	10.9
i	192	24.0
j	14	1.8
n	800	100.0
v	800	100.0
b_2	800	100.0

Appendix

d. Substitutions (MS B)

Table 42

Mss	Total Minority Readings	Total as % of B
B	111	100.0
y	52	46.9
a$_2$	74	66.7
b′	7	6.3
b	11	9.9
o	14	12.6
c$_2$	15	13.5
e$_2$	9	8.1
A	17	15.3
c	15	13.5
x	16	14.4
d	8	7.2
[l	3	2.7]
p	8	7.2
q	8	7.2
t	9	8.1
z	8	7.2
e	13	11.7
f	10	9.0
m	10	9.0
s	10	9.0
w	8	7.2
[M	3	2.7]
N	13	11.7
a	10	9.0
g	13	11.7
h	11	9.9
i	10	9.0
[j	7	6.3]
n	17	15.3
v	11	9.9
b$_2$	9	8.1

e. Transpositions (MS B)

Table 43

Mss	Total Minority Readings	Total as % of B
B	9	100.0
y	8	88.9
a_2	3	33.3
b′	0	
b	0	
o	0	
c_2	0	
e_2	0	
A	0	
c	0	
x	0	
d	0	
l	0	
p	2	22.2
q	0	
t	0	
z	0	
e	1	11.7
f	0	
m	0	
s	0	
w	0	
M	0	
N	0	
a	0	
g	0	
h	1	11.1
i	0	
j	0	
n	2	22.2
v	0	
b_2	0	

f. Additions (MS B)

Table 44

Mss	Total Minority Readings	Total as % of B
B	34	100.0
y	22	64.7
a_2	24	70.6
b'	1	2.9
b	2	5.9
o	2	5.9
c_2	2	5.9
e_2	2	5.9
A	5	14.7
c	9	26.5
x	6	17.7
d	2	5.9
l	1	2.9
p	2	5.9
q	3	8.8
t	3	8.8
z	4	11.8
e	2	5.9
f	1	2.9
m	1	2.9
s	1	2.9
w	1	2.9
M	1	2.9
N	1	2.9
a	3	8.8
g	1	2.9
h	1	2.9
i	2	5.9
j	0	
n	2	5.9
v	2	5.9
b_2	1	2.9

g. *Totals (MS B)*

Table 45

Mss	Total Minority Readings	Total as % of B
B	673	100.0
y	418	62.1
a_2	457	67.9
b′	66	9.8
b	71	10.6
o	81	12.0
c_2	79	11.7
e_2	69	10.3
A	256	38.0
c	202	30.0
x	218	32.4
d	101	15.0
[l	48	7.1]
p	109	16.2
q	113	16.8
t	112	16.6
z	106	15.8
e	161	23.9
f	139	20.7
m	126	18.7
s	136	20.2
w	146	21.7
[M	42	6.2]
N	134	19.9
a	123	18.3
g	80	11.9
h	116	17.2
i	139	20.7
[j	76	11.3]
n	192	28.5
v	95	14.1
b_2	133	19.8

Appendix

Ms A as the collation manuscript
  h. Base Text

Table 46

Mss	Total Minority Readings	Total as % of A
A	250	100.0
c	143	57.2
x	154	61.6
b′	27	10.8
b	22	8.8
o	26	10.4
c_2	25	10.0
e_2	18	7.2
B	233	93.2
y	177	70.8
a_2	188	75.2
d	58	23.2
[l	26	10.4]
p	60	24.0
q	60	24.0
t	61	24.4
z	51	20.4
e	51	20.4
f	47	18.8
m	46	18.4
s	47	18.8
w	52	20.8
[M	15	6.0]
N	47	18.8
a	45	18.0
g	27	10.8
h	35	14.0
i	56	22.4
[j	24	9.6]
n	59	23.6
v	37	14.8
b_2	42	16.8

i. Base Text–hexaplaric (MS A)

Table 47

Mss	Total Minority Readings	Total as % of A
A	92	100.0
c	59	64.1
x	65	70.7
b′	26	28.3
b	24	26.1
o	27	29.4
c_2	26	28.3
e_2	26	28.3
B	0	
y	0	
a_2	2	2.2
d	44	47.9
l	58	63.1
p	58	63.1
q	59	64.1
t	57	62.0
z	58	63.1
e	63	68.5
f	31	33.7
m	29	31.5
s	29	31.5
w	65	70.7
[M	0	]
N	15	16.3
a	0	
g	20	21.7
h	4	4.4
i	4	4.4
j	52	56.5
n	0	
v	0	
b_2	0	

j. Omissions (MS A)

Table 48

Mss	Total Minority Readings	Total as % of A
A	223	100.0
c	119	53.4
x	111	49.8
b′	64	28.7
b	58	26.0
o	59	26.5
c_2	49	22.0
e_2	51	22.9
B	14	6.3
y	41	18.4
a_2	32	14.4
d	54	24.2
[l	11	4.9]
p	31	13.9
q	29	13.0
t	28	12.6
z	41	18.4
e	21	9.4
f	19	8.5
m	18	8.1
s	12	5.4
w	17	7.6
[M	4	1.8]
N	13	5.8
a	35	15.7
g	17	7.6
h	17	7.6
i	22	9.9
[j	7	3.1]
n	14	6.3
v	36	16.1
b_2	9	4.0

k. Substitutions (MS A)

Table 49

Mss	Total Minority Readings	Total as % of A
A	341	100.0
c	151	44.3
x	148	43.4
b′	63	18.5
b	61	17.9
o	59	17.3
c₂	57	16.7
e₂	62	18.2
B	17	5.0
y	45	13.2
a₂	55	16.1
d	86	25.2
[l	52	15.3]
p	95	27.9
q	101	29.6
t	95	27.9
z	82	24.1
e	33	9.7
f	32	9.4
m	26	7.6
s	25	7.3
w	24	7.0
[M	14	4.1]
N	41	12.0
a	45	13.2
g	48	14.1
h	30	8.8
i	38	11.1
[j	15	4.4]
n	33	9.7
v	44	12.9
b₂	31	9.1

l. *Transpositions (MS A)*

Table 50

Mss	Total Minority Readings	Total as % of A
A	115	100.0
c	82	71.3
x	89	77.4
b′	35	30.4
b	40	34.8
o	36	31.3
c₂	39	33.9
e₂	40	34.8
B	0	
y	6	5.2
a₂	1	0.9
d	38	33.0
[l	26	22.6]
p	42	36.5
q	45	39.1
t	46	40.0
z	41	35.7
e	2	1.7
f	8	7.0
m	3	2.6
s	1	0.9
w	1	0.9
[M	1	0.9]
N	1	0.9
a	6	5.2
g	5	4.4
h	1	0.9
i	1	0.9
[j	1	0.9]
n	7	6.1
v	3	2.6
b₂	3	2.6

m. Additions (MS A)

Table 51

Mss	Total Minority Readings	Total as % of A
A	467	100.0
c	322	69.0
x	328	70.2
b′	207	44.3
b	211	45.2
o	202	43.3
c_2	237	50.8
e_2	197	42.2
B	5	1.1
y	17	3.6
a_2	13	2.8
d	179	38.3
[l	101	21.6]
p	213	45.6
q	229	49.0
t	227	48.6
z	255	54.6
e	71	15.2
f	63	13.5
m	59	12.6
s	42	9.0
w	82	17.6
[M	7	1.5]
N	41	8.8
a	15	3.2
g	58	12.4
h	25	5.4
i	40	8.6
[j	19	4.1]
n	29	6.2
v	27	5.8
b_2	14	2.1

n. Totals (MS A)

Table 52

Mss	Total Minority Readings	Total as % of A
A	1173	100.0
c	698	59.5
x	719	61.3
b′	332	28.3
b	334	28.5
o	323	27.5
c_2	358	30.5
e_2	317	27.0
B	255	21.7
y	245	20.9
a_2	257	21.9
d	361	30.8
[l	205	17.5]
p	410	35.0
q	435	37.1
t	429	36.6
z	429	36.6
e	157	13.4
f	150	12.8
m	134	11.4
s	115	9.8
w	159	13.6
[M	37	3.2]
N	130	11.1
a	111	9.5
g	138	11.8
h	91	7.8
i	135	11.5
[j	59	5.0]
n	128	10.9
v	111	9.5
b_2	90	7.7

o. Totals without Additions (MS A)

Table 53

Mss	Total Minority Readings	Total as % of A
A	706	100.0
c	376	53.3
x	391	55.4
b′	125	17.7
b	123	17.4
o	121	17.1
c₂	121	17.1
e₂	120	16.1
B	250	35.4
y	228	32.3
a₂	244	34.6
d	182	25.8
[l	104	14.7]
p	197	27.9
q	206	29.2
t	202	28.6
z	174	24.7
e	86	12.2
f	87	12.3
m	75	10.6
s	73	10.3
w	77	10.9
[M	30	4.3]
N	89	12.6
a	96	13.6
g	80	11.3
h	66	9.4
i	95	13.5
[j	40	5.7]
n	99	14.0
v	84	11.9
b₂	76	10.8

Bibliography of Works Cited

Texts

Brooke, A. E. and McLean, N., with Thackeray, H. St. J., eds. *The Old Testament in Greek According to the Text of Codex Vaticanus, Supplemented from Other Uncial Manuscripts, with a Critical Apparatus Containing the Variants of the Chief Ancient Authorities for the Text of the Septuagint*, Volume 1: *The Octateuch*; Vol. 2: *The later Historical Books*. Cambridge: Cambridge University Press, 1906-27.

Elliger, K., Rudolph, W., et al., eds. *Biblia Hebraica Stuttgartensia*. Stuttgart: Deutsche Bibelstiftung, 1977.

de Lagarde, Paul A., ed. *Librorum Veteris Testamenti canonicorum Pars prior*. Göttingen, 1883.

Rahlfs, Alfred, ed. *Septuaginta, id est Vetus Testamentum graece iuxta LXX interpretes*. 2 vols. 9th ed. Stuttgart: Württembergische Bibelanstalt, (no date).

Reference Works and Studies

Abercrombie, John R. *Computer Programs for Literary Analysis*. Philadelphia: University of Pennsylvania Press, 1984.

_____; Adler, William; Kraft, Robert A.; and Tov, Emanuel. *Computer Assisted Tools for Septuagint Studies*. Vol. 1, Ruth. Atlanta: Scholars Press, 1986.

Abbott-Smith, G. *A Manual Greek Lexicon of the New Testament*. 3rd edition. Edinburgh: T. & T. Clark, 1937.

Barthélemy, Dominique. *Les devanciers d'Aquila. Vetus Testamentum Supplement* 10. Leiden: E. J. Brill, 1963.

_____. "Les problèmes textuels de 2 Sam 11,2-1 Rois 2,11 reconsidérés à la lumière de certaines critiques des 'Devanciers d'Aquila.'" *1972 Proceedings. Septuagint and Cognate Studies* 2. Edited by R. A. Kraft. Missoula: Society of Biblical Literature, 1972: 16-89.

Brock, S. P. "Lucian redivivus: Some Reflections on Barthélemy's Les devanciers d'Aquila." *Studia Evangelica* 5 (1968): 176-181.

_____. "Origen's Aims as a Textual Critic of the Old Testament." *Studies in the Septuagint: Origins, Recensions, and Interpretations.* Edited by H. M. Orlinsky. New York: KTAV Publishing House, 1974: 343-346.

_____. "The Recensions of the Septuagint Version of I Samuel." Unpublished D.Phil. dissertation, Oxford, 1966.

Busto Saiz, J. R. "On the Lucianic Manuscripts in 1-2 Kings." *VI Congress of the International Organization for Septuagint and Cognate Studies.* Edited by Claude E. Cox. Atlanta: Scholars Press, 1987: 305-310.

Conybeare, F. C. and Stock, St. George. *Grammar of Septuagint Greek.* Peabody, Mass.: Hendrickson Publishers, 1988. Reprinted from *Selections from the Septuagint.* Boston: Ginn and Company, 1905.

Cross, Frank Moore. *The Ancient Library of Qumran and Modern Studies.* Revised Edition. Grand Rapids: Baker Book House, 1961.

_____. "The Evolution of a Theory of Local Texts." *Qumran and the History of the Biblical Text.* Edited by F. M. Cross and Shemaryahu Talmon. Cambridge, Mass.: Harvard University Press, 1975: 306-320.

_____. "The History of the Biblical Text in the Light of Discoveries in the Judaean Desert." *Harvard Theological Review* 57 (1964): 281-299.

Dieu, L. "Les manuscripts grecs des Livres de Samuel." *Le Muséon* 24 (1921): 17-60.

Driver, S. R. *Notes on the Hebrew Text and the Topography of the Books of Samuel.* 2nd. edition. Oxford: Clarendon Press, 1913.

Fernández Marcos, N. "Literary and Editorial Features of the Antiochian Text in Kings." *VI Congress of the International Organization for Septuagint and Cognate Studies.* Edited by Claude E. Cox. Atlanta: Scholars Press, 1987: 287-304.

Gooding, D. W. A review of *Chronology and Recensional Development in the Greek Text of Kings,* by J. D. Shenkel, in *Journal of Theological Studies,* n.s. 21 (1970): 118-131.

Holmes, R. and Parsons, J., eds. *Vetus Testamentum graecum cum variis lectionibus.* Vol. 2. Oxford: Clarendon Press, 1810.

Jellicoe, Sidney. "The Hesychian Recension Reconsidered." *The Journal of Biblical Literature* 82 (1963): 409-418.

_____. "Prolegomenon." *Studies in the Septuagint: Origins, Recensions, and Interpretations.* Edited by H. M. Orlinsky. New York: KTAV Publishing House, 1974: xiii-lxii.

_____. *The Septuagint and Modern Study.* Oxford: University Press, 1968; reprint ed., Ann Arbor: Eisenbrauns, 1978.

Johnson, Bo. *Die Hexaplarische Rezension des I. Samuelbuches der Septuaginta.* Lund: C. W. K. Gleerup, 1963.

Kahle, Paul E. *The Cairo Geniza.* 2nd edition. Oxford: Basil Blackwell, 1959.

Katz, P. [See also Walters] "Septuagintal Studies in the Mid-century." *Studies in the Septuagint: Origins, Recensions, and Interpretations.* Edited by H. M. Orlinsky. New York: KTAV Publishing House, 1974: 21-53.

Kraft, Robert A. Review of *Les devanciers d'Aquila,* by D. Barthélemy, in *Gnomon* 37 (1965): 474-483.

_____. "Septuagint: Earliest Greek Versions." *Interpreter's Dictionary of the Bible*. Supplementary Volume. Nashville: Abingdon Press, 1976: 811-815.

Kraft, Robert A., and Tov, Emanuel. "Computer Assisted Tools for Septuagint Studies." *Bulletin of the International Organization for Septuagint and Cognate Studies* 14 (1981): 22-40.

McGarry, W. J. "Early Revisions of the Septuagint Text." *Proceedings of the Catholic Biblical Association of America*. Missouri (1938): 29-35.

Martin, R. A. "Some Syntactical Criteria of Translation Greek." *Vetus Testamentum* 10 (1960): 295-310.

_____. *Syntactical Evidence of Semitic Sources in Greek Documents*. Septuagint and Cognate Studies 3. Missoula: Scholars Press, 1974.

_____. "Syntax Criticism of the LXX Additions to the Book of Esther." *Journal of Biblical Literature* 94 (1975): 65-72.

Metzger, Bruce M. "The Lucianic Recension of the Greek Bible." *Chapters in the History of New Testament Textual Criticism*. New Testament Tools and Studies 4. Leiden: E. J. Brill, 1963: 1-41.

Rahlfs, Alfred. *Studien zu den Königsbüchern*. Septuaginta-Studien 1. Göttingen: Vandenhoeck and Ruprecht, 1901.

_____. *Lucians Rezension der Königsbücher*. Septuaginta-Studien 3. Göttingen: Vandenhoeck and Ruprecht, 1911.

Roberts, Bleddyn J. *The Old Testament Text and Versions*. Cardiff: University of Wales Press, 1951.

Shenkel, J. D. *Chronology and Recensional Development in the Greek Text of Kings*. Harvard Semitic Monographs 1. Cambridge, Mass.: Harvard University Press, 1968.

Skeat, T. C. "The Use of Dictation in Ancient Book-production." *Proceedings of the British Academy* 42 (1956): 179-208.

Swete, H. B. *An Introduction to the Old Testament in Greek.* Cambridge: Cambridge University Press, 1902; reprint ed., New York: KTAV Publishing House, 1968.

Taylor, B. A. "The CATSS Variant Database: An Evaluation." *Bulletin of the International Organization for Septuagint and Cognate Studies* 25 (1992).

Thackeray, H. St. J. *A Grammar of the Old Testament in Greek.* Volume 1: Introduction, orthography and accidence. Cambridge: Cambridge University Press, 1909; reprint ed., Hildesheim: Georg Olms Verlag, 1987.

_____. "The Greek Translators of the Four Books of Kings." *The Journal of Theological Studies* 8 (1907): 262-278.

_____. *The Septuagint and Jewish Worship. A Study in Origins* (Schweich Lectures, 1920). London: Oxford University Press, 1921.

Tov, Emanuel. "Lucian and proto-Lucian--Toward a New Solution of the Problem." *Revue biblique* 79 (1972): 101-113.

_____. "Septuagint." *Interpreter's Dictionary of the Bible.* Supplementary Volume. Nashville: Abingdon Press, 1976: 807-811.

Tsevat, M. "Samuel I, II." *Interpreter's Dictionary of the Bible.* Supplementary Volume. Nashville: Abingdon Press, 1976: 777-781.

Ulrich, E. C. "The Old Latin Translation of the LXX and the Hebrew Scrolls from Qumran." *The Hebrew and Greek Texts of Samuel.* Edited by E. Tov. Jerusalem: Simor Ltd, 1980: 121-165.

_____. *The Qumran Text of Samuel and Josephus.* Harvard Semitic Monographs 19. Chico: Scholars Press, 1978.

Walters, Peter (formerly Katz). *The Text of the Septuagint. Its Corruptions and Their Emendations.* Edited by D. W. Gooding. Cambridge: Cambridge University Press, 1973.

Wevers, J. W. "Proto-Septuagint Studies." *The Seed of Wisdom. Essays in Honour of T. J. Meek.* Edited by W. S. McCullough. Toronto: University Press, 1964: 58-77.

_____. "Septuagint." *The Interpreter's Dictionary of the Bible.* Nashville: Abingdon Press, 1962. 4:273-278.

_____. "Text History and Text Criticism of the Septuagint." *Vetus Testamentum* 29 (1977): 392-402.

www.ingramcontent.com/pod-product-compliance
Lightning Source LLC
Chambersburg PA
CBHW032029120726
47901CB00002BA/661